SPACE TOYS OF THE 60's

An Illustrated Collector's Guide To

MAJOR MATT MASON,

ZEROID ROBOTS AND STAR TEAM,

AND

COLORFORMS OUTER SPACE MEN

By James H. Gillam

Space Toys Of The 60's

An Illustrated Collector's Guide To

Major Matt Mason,
Zeroid Robots and STAR TEAM,

And

Colorforms Outer Space Men

By James H. Gillam

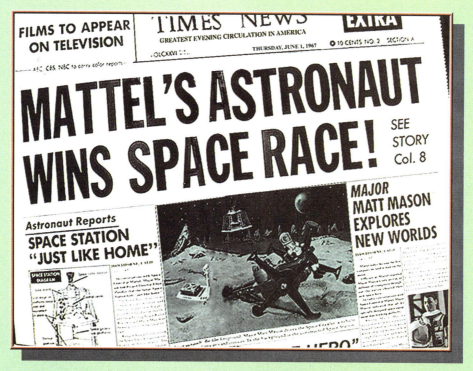

Space Toys of the 60's by James H. Gillam
ISBN 1-896522-37-8

~~~ Contents ~~~

Acknowledgments

I would like to thank the following people who, over the past ten years, have made this book possible through their invaluable knowledge, insight and perseverance in collecting and preserving the memory of Major Matt Mason, Mighty Zeroid Robots and STAR Team, and Colorforms Outer Space Men toys. These people have, in many cases, helped to re-ignite an interest in these long lost toys which bring back many happy memories of a carefree childhood. And thanks, of course, to Mom and Dad, who really got me started on Major Matt Mason and Mighty Zeroid robots when I was eight years old, and to Skip, who has accompanied me to countless toy fairs and smiled through each and every one of them. A special note of thanks to both James Molina, an "expert" on Zeroid toys, and Larry Chinn, one of a handful of Major Matt Mason authorities. This book wouldn't have been possible, or at least would have been a lot less interesting, without their assistance and patience. I'd also like to pay thanks to John Eaton, Ray Kolasa, Don Thompson, Keith Myers, Christian De Grandpre, Claude Switzer, and Mark Stuart. Thanks as well to Craig Galassi who did the work of photographing my private collection to be used in this book. Special thanks to Robert Godwin who suggested that I write this book in the first place; not only is he my publisher, but he and I go a long way back in collecting, among other things, Major Matt Mason.

Introduction

This book is a collector's guide to *Major Matt Mason: Mattel's Man In Space*, *Mighty Zeroid Robots* and *STAR TEAM* from Ideal Toys, and Colorform Toys *Outer Space Men*.

The Mattel *Man In Space* series of toys was manufactured from 1966 through 1970 and featured dozens of toys including "bendie" astronauts, aliens, playsets, individual accessories and space vehicles. Variations, copies and unique items continued to appear in foreign markets for some time after that — Larry Chinn of San Francisco recently discovered a Canadian-only *Astro Trac* Gift Set and *Scorpio* is reported to have had his own *Command Center* available only in some European and Latin Markets. New discoveries continue to be made, so this book cannot be the definitive guide to *Major Matt Mason* toys. There is no worldwide master list of toys produced and neither is an archive available. There has been speculation that some toys shown in dealer catalogues were not actually produced or were produced only in extremely small numbers — *Or* and his *Orbitor* being a case in point. This book does cover virtually all of Mattel's known production from both the United States of America and Canada. It also covers manufacturing that occurred in Latin America, Germany, Britain and Italy.

In 1967, The Ideal Toy Company introduced the *Mighty Zeroid Robots*. *Zeroids* were perfect companions for *Matt Mason*, standing about an inch taller at 6½" to 7" high. Both physically and visually *Zeroids* complemented *Matt Mason* and his accessories, so that toys from these two lines were often found together, embarking side-by-side on missions designed by school-aged aspiring astronauts. In 1970, Ideal added their *STAR TEAM* line of Space Exploration Gear toys, but, by this time, interest in space was ebbing, so that the *STAR TEAM* line was produced for only about a year. Being associated with *Zeroids*, the *STAR TEAM* toys are also included in this guide.

Seeing the popularity of *Matt Mason* and *Zeroid Robots*, in 1968 The Colorform Company created its own line of bendable rubber alien figures — *Outer Space Men*. These unusual figures ranged in height from the 3" *Alpha 7* (from Venus) to 7" *Colossus Rex* (from Jupiter.) Colorform Toys introduced the seven *Outer Space Men* figures in 1968. These toys were more imaginative than *Matt Mason* and *Zeroids*, which were more closely tied to real world designs, and the packaging artwork for the Colorform toys was always great.

This collector's guide presents the details of these very special toys from a special time — a time long gone, but still remembered, and still cherished. Enjoy.

Part 1 - Space Toys Of The 60's

A Guide To The Adventure Of Collecting

Why do we collect things, toys, stamps, soda bottles, and coins, shoes and old cloths? Because it has many rewards. Finding that rare and elusive item after days, months or sometimes years of searching is self-satisfying — it's the thrill of the hunt, and the delight of finding that "deal to end all deals." Collecting can be a great hobby and affords the collector the experience of meeting other collectors. Shared experiences, value of collectable items, discussions of variations and rare pieces add to the fun and enjoyment of meeting with like-minded people. Each item that is found — whether by scouring flea markets, winning in auctions, buying from ads in newspapers, or over the marketing wave of the future, the Internet — becomes a trophy of perseverance and dedication to an elite group of hobbyists.

I have amazed myself over the years with what I've personally collected, and have come to realize that virtually everything has value to someone and is most probably collectable. Finally, the beauty of collecting is that, unlike consumer disposable items that have no value after purchase, collectibles can always be sold to someone else. Collections are often moved on from person to person, and upgrading to higher quality items frequently occurs as collectors become more experienced.

The following outline, it is my hope, will provide a guideline for collecting the many Mattel *Man In Space* toys, *Mighty Zeroid Robots* made by the Ideal Toy company, and Colorform Toys *Outer Space Men*.

Who Buys Old Space Toys?

The people who collect *Major Matt Mason*, *Zeroids* and *Outer Space Men* toys fall into a number of clearly defined categories:

1. People who buy them as a toy or collectable item because they had these toys as young children, and most often have fond memories of a particular toy (the category that I as a collector fall into.) Memories often include television commercials and advertising that "sold" the toy.
2. People who are interested in Space and the Space Program (NASA). They may also have a general interest in Science Fiction. The collecting of space toys frequently complements their interest in Space.
3. Although most people collect these toys as a result of childhood experiences and as a hobby, some may also collect as a means of financial investment.

4. Finally, some people collect these items strictly as dealers and investors. Their intent is solely to realize a profit from their knowledge of these toys and develop a network of buyers to supply these collectable toys to.

A short time ago a questionnaire was circulated, throughout the Internet, among various *Major Matt Mason* toy collectors. The results are enlightening and you may find yourself reflected in the data here, I know I did.

The average age of a collector is between 36 and 40. Most collectors of these toys are male and married. It was found that they primarily live in their own house. They generally played with Major Matt Mason and Zeroids as a child. The male collector has been collecting items from these toy lines for the past three years. These men reported that, when they were children, their favorite and most memorable toys were: *Major Matt Mason, G.I Joe, Hot Wheels, Thingmaker, Slotcars* and *Viewmaster*. Most men use the Internet to purchase toys and read toy-collecting publications. Respondents all reported watching horror sci-fi as children. They generally listen to pop music. For interest, I have provided a percentage breakdown of the questionnaire results.

Age:
- 26-30 yrs..........44 %
- 36- 40 yrs ....50 %
- 41-46 yrs........... 6 %

Gender:
- Male...................100 %

Marital Status:
- Married..............70 %
- Single.................30 %

Area of the USA Where You Grew Up:
- West ....22 %
- East....................39 %
- South................. 6 %
- North ....33 %

Type of Housing:
- House ....89 %
- Apart.................11 %

How Long Have You Been Collecting Major Matt Mason:
- 1 year or less...28%
- 2-3 years 33%
- 4-7 years 17%
- 8-10 years........11%
- 10+ years..........11%

How Many Items Are In Your Major Matt Mason Collection:
- Up to 10 ....22 %
- 11-30.................33 %
- 31-75.................11 %
- 76-125 ....17 %
- 126-200 ....17 %

Toys Played With As A Child:
- G.I Joe...............60 %
- Zeroid Robots.55 %
- Captain Action.20 %
- Hot Wheels......85 %
- Thingmaker ......75 %
- Slotcars.............70 %
- Viewmaster ......80 %

Occupation:
Technical ....61 %

Business.............28 %
Marketing..........11 %

Type of TV Shows You Watched As A Child:
sci-fi Horror.....100 %

Do You Consider Yourself To Be Retentive:
Yes ....95 %
No .... 5 %

Annual Income:
Up to 25,000....6 %
25,000-75,000..38 %
75,000-125,00038 %
125,000+...........18 %

Type of Car You Drive:
Compact ....17 %
Sedan ....17 %
Luxury ....22 %
Sports Car........11 %
SUV ....33 %

Do You Collect Any Other Toys Today:
G.I Joe...............25 %
Zeroid Robots.40 %
Captain Action.25 %
Hot Wheels......15 %
Thingmaker ......10 %

How To Use This Reference Guide

Space Toys Of The 60's was designed to be an authoritative and easy to use collector's guide. It is divided into three parts — *Major Matt Mason*, *Zeroid Robots* and *STAR TEAM*, and *Colorforms Outer Space Men* — each of which is then organized into meaningful chapter-like sections. Within the product detail and pricing sections, individual toys are identified by their official names, and for the *Matt Mason* and *Zeroids* toys the stock numbers used by Mattel and Ideal respectively are also used. The stock numbers have been used as an unambiguous identification system, allowing specific information to be located quickly and easily. Throughout the guide, pictures and illustrations have been included adjacent to their relevant text and are labeled by toy name along with stock numbers for the Mattel and Ideal toys.

Condition Of Collectable Toys

This reference guide uses three defining categories for toys based on their presentation, which may ultimately dictate not only the monetary value, but also the collectability of the toy. Having said that, beauty is most definitely in the eye of the beholder. When money becomes involved however, we may view toys through rose colored glasses or with x-ray vision, depending on our particular need. A seller may view that collectable toy as perfect and charge accordingly. The potential toy collector may view the toy as suspect. What is clear, however, is that there should be a large spread monetarily between a "mint in boxed" toy and a "loose" toy. The definitions that are used in this guide are as follows:

Mint

A mint toy is complete with all the accessories and decals that were included at the point of manufacture. It will be in unplayed-with condition, thereby being "like new." That being said, I would hazard to say that a mint toy does not look like it was used, has no (non-factory) defects, scratches, wear and tear, broken or damaged edges, cracks or splits.

Mint in Box (MIB) Mint on Card (MOC)

A mint in box or mint on card toy meets the above description and in addition is complete with either the original box or card. The box or card is to be in mint "like new" condition, as is the toy. A box that is dented or has a torn end flap, or a card that has had a bubble re-glued or partially removed in not a MIB or MOC item.

Loose

A loose and played with toy is not a mint toy. As such, it will be of lesser value than the above mentioned toys. That's not to say that loose toys have no value. If a toy is loose, but is in high demand, it may in fact have great value as the marketplace will dictate. Loose toys may not have decals or they may be worn. These toys may not have all the initially included accessories. The toy may be worn with scratches and show "play." The range between loose toys will vary. A good loose toy will be worth more than a similar fair or poor condition loose toy.

Caring For Collectable Toys

All *Major Matt Mason* figures, *Mighty Zeroid Robots*, *Outer Space Men* figures, action playsets and accessories are made of rubber and plastic. Soft plastics and rubber such as those used to mold our brave *Major*, and the hard plastic used to mold the *Mighty Zeroid* are highly susceptible to the sunlight — specifically ultraviolet light. With over-exposure to UV light (perhaps the toy sits near a sunny window) over time the toy's plastic will undergo chemical reactions. The compound of the plastic may become hard and brittle, pieces may melt, bodies may crack, paint may fade and colors will change. *Major Matt Mason* more than *Zeroids* will suffer chemical reaction damage unless treated carefully. You may notice when looking at your orange *Talking Backpack*, perhaps even the one in your mint *Talking Flying Major Matt Mason Glider* box, for example, that despite the toy never having been out of the box, the pack appears to have melted. You may find this on *Matt Mason* hands, *Space Sleds*, and even *Callisto*'s purple sensor. The rubber used to mold *Matt Mason* and his *Space Exploration Team* breaks down over time and creates a chemical reaction with harder plastics. This is especially true of the unpainted black rubber parts.

How do you, as a collector, protect your toys? The easiest way is to remove your figures from direct contact with their hard plastic accessories and, at all cost, keep them away from ultra-violet light sources. It's important to note that when packing your toys for safe keeping, the rubber compound used for *Major Matt Mason* cannot come into contact with any type of Styrofoam packing. The packing chips (peanuts) or any Styrofoam product will almost immediately melt and adhere itself to the *Major*'s rubber painted body and accordion joints. This will most definitely damage the figure and is not removable or reversible. If you choose to pack *Major Matt* in Styrofoam, ensure that he is well wrapped in plastic (baggies work best) and then the chips can be used. Secondly, toys will age less when stored or displayed in cool dry places away from direct heat or dampness. Finally basements and attics are not ideally suited to store these toys. As an example of the effects that environment can have, *Astro Trac* vehicles are rarely found in the southern states with their rear foam wheels intact, but are commonly found in northern states with their rear wheels. Heat and humidity do affect toys drastically, so caution must be taken.

Memories - The Way We Are

If you're reading this sentence, you're probably already a member of the fraternity of die-hard space toy collectors, so you know that there are others out there who feel the same way you do. Odds are, you've often talked with other collectors, comparing notes and memories. What follows are some personal reminiscences from some of the other space toy collectors that I've been lucky enough to encounter in my travels. I'll bet that some of their memories (past and present) will spark memories of your own experiences.

* * * * *

I'm 36 and grew up in central Florida at the height of the space race. Luckily for me, my Dad was into the developing space program and everything that was going on at Cape Canaveral. At one time I had just about every *MMM* toy made. Unfortunately, over time they didn't survive trips to the beach or the sand pile — my two favorite places to play with my *MMM* stuff. Fast forward to 1998. I was listening to a local consumer advocate on the radio one day and a caller asked about an antique toy. The toy was a *Matt Mason* doll and he wondered about it's value. I must have had some repressed memories because, as soon as I heard this, the search was on. Unfortunately for me, my wife doesn't get it, and has me on a very short leash. I guess that's probably a good thing, because I would have emptied my 401K by now on *MMM* purchases.

* * * * *

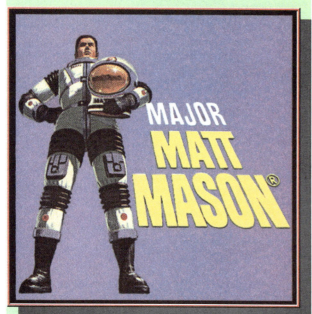

I am 36 and didn't have *MMM* as a kid — my parents got me *G.I. Joe*, but my neighbor had lots-o-*Matt* and it was my favorite thing to play with. I started looking for *MMM* when I was 16 and only found one *Matt*, at an old

antique barn. He was in very sad shape and was marked $40.00 so I passed. My wife doesn't understand, but does put up with my new obsession — she's trying to put me on a one a month purchase plan. Unfortunately, there are some deals I just can't pass up!

* * * * *

I'm 35 years old and got into it at the tail end of *Matt Mason* in 1970-71. I had a [*Space*] *Station*, the figures, a *Glider*, *Starseeker* and the *Power Paks*. I now have just about everything but a *Glider* and *Starseeker*. Since 1982 I had been looking for *MM*, but didn't find it until I came across an ad in a toy magazine four years ago. What amazed me were the vehicles. Since *Matt* was discontinued when I was just starting to play with him, I'd never seen *Scorpio*, the *Astro Trac*, and others. I managed to get a lot of the stuff on trade by swapping all of my Uncle's (he's 39) *GI Joe* toys, which he gave to me. I've also been working on *MM* repairs for those four years, after being told that there was a big demand for how to fix broken wires. Recently my big find was discovering the original paint that Mattel used on the figures.

* * * * *

Matt was my favorite toy when I was a kid. I also had *Zeroids*, a few *Colorforms Aliens*, and then I got into *GI Joe AT* (because *Matt* was no longer available.) My dad loved the entire space program. My grandmother owned a trailer park a few miles from the Cape and my father took me to KSC numerous times when we were on vacation. I count myself fortunate to have seen two *Saturn V* launches from close up (we got passes from friends who were engineers.) Once, in 1975 when I was in Florida on vacation, I found (at the toy store in Merritt Square Mall) a *Space Power Suit* for 99 cents. Someone had discovered it in the back stockroom.

I'm not a purist when it comes to Matt — all of my figures are rewired, but with original paint. Most of my vehicles are broken. I like repairing and customizing the items with original NASA stickers, etc. I have a few original boxes. I don't like clutter, so I only have a *Matt* on a *Sled* and *DD* in *Talking Pack* sitting on my desk next to the computer. When we have more room, maybe I'll put out a *Crawler*. My boss at my part time job has a *Crawler* and *Matt* that I got for him on his shelf.

The best parts of the collecting have been finding my first item, and the friends that I've made. My wife really likes this stuff. I also found last week a *GI Joe Masterpiece Astronaut*. I've been able to spend a minimum, as I've sold repair videos, and got in when the *Matt* craze was just starting, and cheap.

For me *Matt* is everything that this country could be if we had the foresight and commitment. When I was 10, the world wasn't flat. Sadly, it seems that it is for most of the kids I know now.

* * * * *

I fall right in the established age group — 38 pushing 10 — and I'm a single father of three (who live with me.) For years I would mention the *Major* and get blank stares.

I got into collecting the *Major* in a round-about way. I'm heavily into model building. Also, I figured there was no way I'd ever be able to own again what I'd had as a child. So, I thought if I could locate just one figure, I could make a mold and then make all the others and build dioramas for my model contests. That way I could show all the people who had such blank stares about the *Major*. When I got my first figure (my second childhood) I was so proud, that I couldn't wait to show my children, and the first thing out of their mouths was "It's just a Space Man! It doesn't even have a micro chip for sounds!" Needless to say, they now show respect for those "Space Men" in the Domed Display Cases.

I collect many things, but I'm not into resale. I just collect what I had as a child and what is special to me. My children and I have *Star Trek* (Mego, Galloob, Trendmasters all sizes, over a 100+ carded), 12" *G.I. Joes* (mostly commemorative.) *Star Wars* (1977 through New releases), *Godzilla* (my passion) and the other Toho

Monsters, and plastic models (400+ unbuilt, with the delusion of building them all.) And that's not to even mention *Barbie* and *Beanies*!. One thing I've learned — my children won't ever have to worry about Dad throwing out their toys!

* * * * *

I'm 34 years old and had a number of *Matts* when I was a child, mostly *Matt* himself along with a *Storm*, *Lazer*, *Callisto* and *Scorpio*. I also remember clearly having a few Colorform aliens, *Colossus Rex*, *Cmdr. Comet*, *Astro-Nautilus*, and *Alpha 7*. Vehicle-wise I had a *Space Crawler*, a *Bubble* and a *Uni-Tred*. I won the *Uni-Tred* in a church fair when I was young, and I was very excited because it came with a new *Matt* — all mine at the time were "used", to say the least. Let me clarify that it wasn't packaged with *Matt*, but a carded *Matt* figure was part of the prize. Years passed, and after many moves and yard sales, my *Matt* collection had dispersed to the four winds.

* * * * *

I remember my mom taking me to the Emporium at Christmas time, pretending to buy some *Matt* figures for another little boy. She asked me which one I would like, and I told her that *Matt* and "red" guy would be good, but for some reason, she bought two Matts, and gave them to me for Christmas. I also remember a trip to Sacramento to visit my grandmother's sister. I was staying there for a week and had nothing to do. She took me to the toy store and said I could choose any toy I wanted, but only one. I took forever to choose, but eventually settled on the *Firebolt Space Cannon*, the only vehicle that I had as a kid. I loved that thing — the turret blazing, and the sounds that it made! The sad thing is that I don't know what eventually happened to it, when I outgrew toys.

* * * * *

I'm 41 and I grew up in England where the *Major* began showing up around the end of 1968, when I was about 12. I vaguely remember the *Crawler* commercial being shown on UK TV, but *MMM* wasn't the raging success that it was in the US. There were a lot of carded figures and sets available (mostly *Matt* and *Storm*), but the boxed, motorized pieces were few and far between — probably because they were so expensive and the UK economy was way below the US at the time.

I began collecting *Major Matt* again around 1987, back when "common" figures and accessories were fairly inexpensive. For some reason, very few *MMM* pieces or *Colorform Aliens* show up in Canada (where I now live), so most of my collection was acquired south of the border. About the only accessory that I need to finish up my collection now is the green Chest Pak / Gun for *Scorpio*, (Yeah, I know, me and a hundred other collectors.)

* * * * *

I'm 37 and I've been collecting *MMM* for the past five years. I've collected comic books, magazines and any related paper since I was a kid. I've sold my comic collection several times (the first was when I was in college and the *X-Men* became super valuable. I actually financed myself for a year at the University of Tennessee

by selling my collection in 1982), and more recently I sold everything except my magazines, my *Conan* collection and my *Flaming Carrot* comics three years ago. My girlfriend and I were traveling to Clarksville, Tennessee (where I grew up) and made a pit stop right outside of Monteagle, TN. We walked through an open air flea market and I found a small *Shogun Warrior* toy for 25 cents. We became separated and later when she walked up to me she said "Look at this cool astronaut that I just bought for $3. Did I get a good deal?", my heart almost fell out of my mouth! Here was something I hadn't seen, nor realized that I'd missed, since I was 6 or 7 years old! A *Major Matt Mason* wearing a *Talking Back Pack*! I begged her to sell him to me and after a little coercion (which cost me a beautiful 60's "Combat" bagatelle) we managed to work a trade.

The *MMM* was a C7 figure with unbroken wires (most of the paint loss was around the belt from the strap), the *Back Pack* had melt marks, but still worked. This discovery led to the infatuation I have with the little *Major* today. I started my web site about four years ago, So, am I trying to recapture my childhood? I really don't know how to answer that. I'm the real completist (it probably comes from collecting comic books) and have the need to own everything. I've taken it to the extreme, looking for print ads, industry magazines and Christmas catalogues. I'm probably about as nuts as a collector can be, and I know I'm not alone! I know of at least ten others who are as crazy as I am!

* * * * *

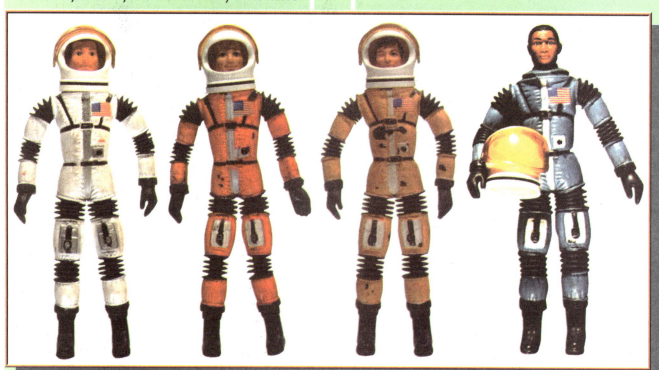

MAJOR MATT MASON

Mattel's
Man In Space

Major Matt Mason Mattel's Man in Space (Mattel Toys)

The History Of Mattel Toys

"One small step for Man, One giant leap for Man in Space"

The year was 1962, Tony Bennett had just won a Grammy award for best record — *I Left My Heart In San Francisco* — Marilyn Monroe had passed away at the age of 36, and *Lawrence of Arabia* was the box office smash hit. The Cuban Missile Crisis had been making the headlines around the world. But on February 20, 1962, John Glenn, aboard Friendship 7, America's first astronaut to go into space, circled the earth three times in four hours and fifty-five minutes at an attitude of 162.2 miles. What would later be coined the "Space Race" to the moon had begun. Americans would no longer dream of flying to the stars, but would, in a few scant years, beat the Soviet Union and be the first to land a man on another celestial body. A frenzied craze had begun and everybody wanted in on the act. Advertising companies were paid millions of dollars to link consumer products — Tang, Spam and *Popsicle Pete* the Rocket Man — to the new great adventures awaiting mankind in outer space. This is what Mattel had been waiting for. It marked their emergence into the US market with a sure fire hit, a true boy's space toy. Mattel would successfully ride the wave of excitement and fervor created by the coming space and moon missions, marking it with a new line of toys including every little boy's very own *Man in Space, Major Matt Mason*.

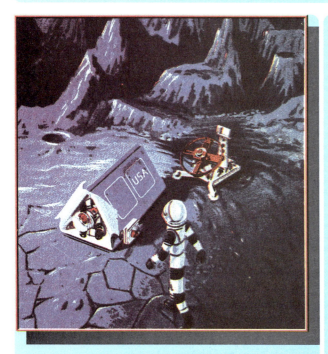

Mattel Toys began producing simple toys in the early 1940's. By 1943 Ruth and Elliot Handler's company was reported to be grossing two million dollars in annual

MATTEL'S MAN IN SPACE

sales. The Mattel Toy company was actually an offshoot of their original company, which produced jewelry and gifts. Mattel Toys was founded by Ruth and Elliot in cooperation with an early business partner, Harold "Matt" Matson (note the similarity to the name of our favorite *Man in Space* action figure.) The new company, whose name came from Harold's nick name "Matt", began producing doll house furniture and then, later on, the Uke-A-Doodle and Burp Gun. After its inception and prior to the production of the most successful toy in history, *Barbie*, Mattel was known for producing conventional toys. Of course, the runaway success that became *Barbie* provided Mattel Toys with enormous income, $25 million in the first two years of production. Incidentally, Ruth and Elliot had two children by then, a daughter and a son, Barbara and Ken.

The Handlers were terrific business people and, with the aid of a large and experienced research and development department, pioneered many of the

Barbie and *G.I. Joe* — Mattel and Hasbro success stories

until the words Gemini and Apollo became part of our everyday vocabulary. The coming moon missions provided the perfect opportunity to introduce a new line of space toys, one that not only seized the imagination of American little boys, but gripped the entire world. The excitement and anticipation of sending the first group of brave men into the cold and dangerous reaches of outer space was both thrilling and terrifying. *Major Matt Mason* would follow in their footsteps and lead the world's children into outer space through vivid imagery, fantastic toys (based originally on "official NASA designs") and box artwork that fueled the imagination.

Talking Flying Major Matt Mason with pull string voice actuation

innovations in toys still used to this day. Mattel was the first company, in the 1960's, to take full advantage of toy technology combined with suave marketing to sign with Walt Disney to provide commercials shown during the TV mega-hit The Mickey Mouse Club. Superior products and a willingness to take substantial risks has kept this company alive while the other three dominant 1960's toy companies were forced to closed their doors. Remco, Marx and Ideal Toys (maker of the *Mighty Zeroid Robots*) are alas no more. To understand the early successes of Mattel Toys we need look no further than their 1960's and early 1970's production line-up including:

Luvvy Duvvy Kiddles,   *Sweet-Treat Kiddles,*
Kosmic Kiddles,   *Kiddle Kolognes,*
Jewelry Kiddles,   *Zoolery Kiddles,*
Animal Kiddles,   *Skediddle Kiddles,*
Buffy and Mrs. Beasley, *Kola Kiddles,*
See 'N Say Talking Storybooks, *Mattel-o-Phones,*
Jack-In-The-Boxes,   *Baby First Step,*
ThingMaker Toys,   *Zoofie-Gooflies,*
Creepy Crawlers,   *Hot Wheels,*
ThingMaker Fun Flowers, *Strange Change Toy,*
Wiz-z-Zer Whirlers,   *Sizzlers,*
Sea Devils.

Mattel was the first company to introduce talking pull-string operated voice boxes for their toys. These boxes were successfully used in, among other Mattel toys, the *Talking Flying Major Matt Mason* and *Command Console*. Prior to the 1960's, Mattel had been producing *Barbie*, but had yet to capture the imagination of little boys —

Major Matt Mason, a white rubber bendie figure dressed in a molded white space suit, led the lineup. He was sold with numerous accessories that continued to grow in diversity and complexity over the life of this line. His *Space Mission Team,* — *Sgt. Storm, Doug Davis,* and *Jeff Long* — joined him after the first year of production. Based on real NASA designs, *Major Matt* and his accessories looked the part. The true to life NASA designed Gemini space suits and the futuristic *Uni-Tred* and *Space Bubble, Astro Trac* and *Firebolt Space Cannon* added a science fiction twist, mixing fantasy play with a dose of realism. The *Space Station* is likely to bring back vivid memories to *Major Matt Mason* fans. Who could forget the more than two foot tall, orange girded *Station*, with flashing purple beacon. It's design allowed for multiple configurations and if you could talk your parents into more than one, you were on your way to building an entire moon colony!

Part 2 - *Major Matt Mason*: Mattel's *Man In Space*

The NASA designed suit on which *Matt Mason's Moon Suit* was based

The *Astro Trac Missile Convoy* set is one of the most difficult items to find. It consisted of the truly rare *Launch Pads* that supported the *Rocket Launch*, *Satellite Launch* and *Space Probe Paks*. They were transported across many a lunarscape or sandbox by the (equally hard to find with rear wheels intact) *Astro Trac*. Unfortunately as the excitement in the NASA Space Program began to wane in the early 1970's, so did the sales of Mattel's *Man In Space* toys. In fact, a fellow collector friend recalls that, in early 1970 at the Hedassa Bizarre in Toronto Canada, Mattel had donated what he recalls as "hundreds" of *Major Matt Mason* mint-in-boxed toys and figures. He convinced his mother to spend the asking price of one dollar per boxed toy and purchased virtually the entire line-up of toys, including the infamous and scary Scorpio figure. I did not attend the Hedassa Bizarre that day. However, just a few short miles away, I was able to pick out my favorite *Major Matt Mason* toys from the local toy store, which, at Christmas in 1970, converted its entire

ground floor level to an other-worldly planetary surface. *Matt Mason* glowed from the shelves and on the huge *Lunar Base* set up in the middle of the "planet display" under the glow of a ceiling full of black lights, a vivid memory I have to this day. On the crater-potted purple-cast moon, all of the vehicles operated — *Space Crawler, Uni-Tred, Space Bubble, Reconojet,* and a huge multi-level *Space Station* and motorized pulley motorific engine enabling both *Reconojet* and *Space Sled* to travel across its ghostly surface. More than thirty years have passed since the onset of Mattel's *Major Matt Mason, Man in Space* production, and collecting the *Major* and his friends, both alien and human, is at an all time high. Today, toys and figures can still be found intact and, in some cases, in working condition. The indestructible *Space Crawler, Uni-Tred* and *Space Bubble* to name a few.

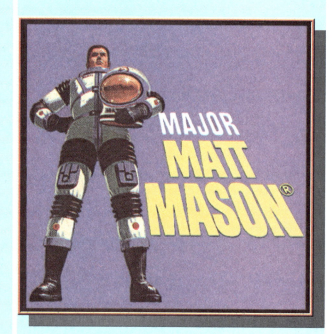

Today's toy makers could learn a thing or two from the inventiveness of Mattel.

Part 2 - *Major Matt Mason:* Mattel's *Man In Space*

The Major Matt Mason 1967-1970 Product Line

As noted in earlier chapters, Mattel's *Major Matt Mason* line of toys was loosely based on the United States Space Program and specifically the Gemini and Apollo manned NASA space missions.

The following chapter itemizes each of the toys in the *Major Matt Mason* toy line. Each toy is identified by stock number and official name. Details of the toy, figure and/or accessory items included in the box or on the blister card are provided along with a packaging description. Where available, a picture of the exterior of the box or blister card is included (for easy reference) as well as the contents of the carded or boxed set.

Note that this chapter doesn't include foreign toys, which are covered separately later in the book.

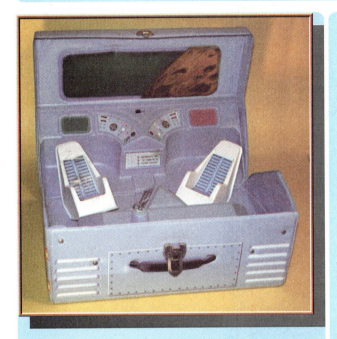

Stock Number: 5157
Item Name: *Talking Command Console*
Copyright Date: 1968
Contents:

"Mattel's First Talking Space Toy". This black strapped carrying case / play station was a "talkie", speaking ten different phrases when the console white-ringed cord was pulled. It included "real space sounds" as well. When the batteries were installed the "interior radar screens light with flashing colored signals." The case included two swivel / tilt astronaut couches that fit *Major Matt Mason* and *Callisto* "bendie's".

Accessories:
None.

Packaging:
This was a beautiful litho vinyl case with interior space ship detailing. The exterior was highly illustrated and included a clear "vista" window with a large graphic of the moon to the left side. This item was sold separately and measured 14" x 9" x 3".

Stock Number: 6300
Item Name: *Major Matt Mason Flight Pak*
Copyright Date: 1966
Contents:

A white *Major Matt Mason* toy figure, helmet, two piece *Space Sled*, *Jet Propulsion Backpack*, and *Space Sled* decal sheet.

Packaging:
Bubble blister card 10" x 13".

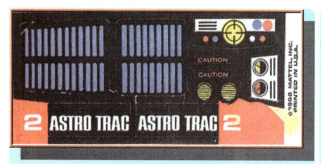

Decals for #6302 *Astro Trac* (below)

Decals for #6300 *Major Matt Mason Flight Pak* (previous page)

Stock Number: 6301
Item Name: *Moon Suit Pak*
Copyright Date: 1966
Contents:

A molded white plastic dome-type suit with attached accordion flexible rubber arms, clear tubing and yellow bellow comprises the number 3 *Moon Suit* based on NASA designs.

Accessories:

Chromed plastic hammer, wrench, screwdriver and molded two piece with black thread radiation detector with decal sheet.

Packaging:

Bubble blister card - 8½" x 12".

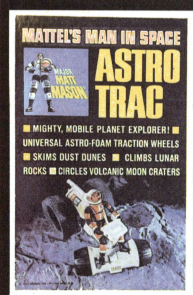

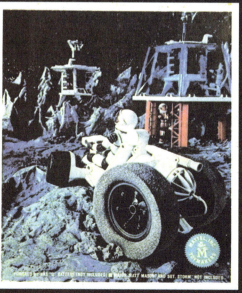

Stock Number: 6302
Item Name: *Astro Trac*
Copyright Date: 1966
Contents:

White plastic battery powered one man "mobile explorer." This vehicle was 7" long and featured "front wheels that steer" and "Astro foam rear wheels" and included a decal sheet.

Packaging:

Boxed item - 14" x 9" x 7".

Part 2 - *Major Matt Mason*: Mattel's *Man In Space*

Stock Number: 6303
Item Name: **Major Matt Mason with Moon Suit**
Copyright Date: 1966
Contents:
  White *Major Matt Mason* figure, helmet, *Jet Pak*, *Moon Suit* that snaps over *Matt* and "features attachable air pump for remote control arm movement", two piece *Space Sled*, two piece radiation detector, "chromed" wrench, screw driver and rock hammer.
Packaging:
  Bubble blister card - 13" x 14".

Stock Number: 6304
Item Name: **Space Crawler**
Copyright Date: 1966
Contents:
  The gray plastic vehicle with four rotating spider wheels was loosely based on a NASA design. This "invincible vehicle tracks over the roughest terrain and always lands on its rotating legs" and features 2-way gears that enable it to operate a winch. It comes complete with red hook, red rolling rear wheel, red toggle and red radar-type switches. A decal sheet is included with the *Space Crawler*.
Packaging:
  Boxed item - 14" x 9" x 9".

Stock Number: 6305
Item Name: **Rocket Launch Pak**
Copyright Date: 1966
Contents:
  A defense weapon which includes a two-piece silver-colored remote controlled rocket launcher utilizing a spring mechanism to fire a red missile.
Accessories:
  Rotojet gun (similar design to the *Lost in Space* gun), two walkie-talkies, knife and sheath, belt and decals.
Packaging:
  Bubble blister card - 8½" x 12".

Part 2 - Major Matt Mason: Mattel's *Man In Space*

Decals for #6305 *Rocket Launch Pak* (previous page)

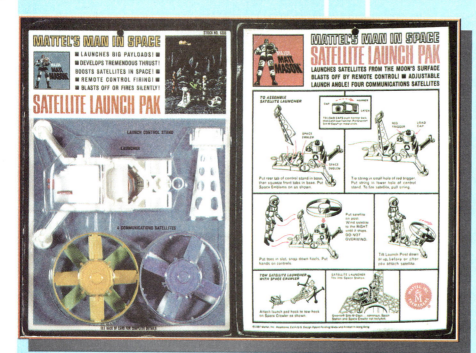

Stock Number: 6306
Item Name: *Satellite Launch Pak*
Copyright Date: 1967
Contents:

A white molded plastic two-piece *Satellite Launcher* with four "communication satellites", which were actually round disk projectiles. Each pak came with four *satellites*, one each molded in white, green, blue and yellow. The firing mechanism was able to pivot and shoot off the disks. A decal sheet was included.

Packaging:

Bubble blister card - 8½" x 12".

Stock Number: 6307
Item Name: *Space Probe Pak*
Copyright Date: 1967
Contents:

A silver molded remote control launch base and turret. This item included an adjustable launcher sitting on a ladder type assembly and flexible rubber hose attachment.

Accessories:

Two remote control space probes, water-shooting decontamination laser type rifle, binoculars and flare gun.

Packaging:

Bubble blister card - 8½" x 12".

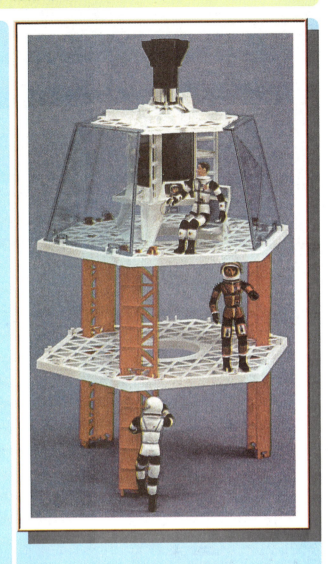

Stock Number: 6308
Item Name: ***Space Station***
Copyright Date: 1966
Contents:

   The *Space Station* is a highly detailed set which comes
   with many parts often missing and/or damaged. The
   Station is made up of the following pieces: white
   molded roof, black and silver beacon, purple beacon
   light cover, transparent instrument panel, 3 command
   center supports, shelf, command desk, three desk
   legs, one pivoting chair, chromed microphone, 3
   chromed "locking bolts", two white hexagon space
   floor platforms, 6 orange support girders, and 6 clear
   blue space panels.

Packaging:

   Boxed item.

Stock Number: 6310
Item Name: ***Space Station Crawler***
                 Deluxe Action Set
Copyright Date: 1966
Contents:

   The *Space Station Crawler Deluxe
   Action Set* was the first toy
   packaged by the Mattel company
   for the Mattel *Man in Space* line.
   It contained items which were
   already sold separately including
   "*Space   Station*:   moon
   headquarters with flashing space
   radar beacon", "motorized *Space
   Crawler* with powerful hoist and
   winch", *Major Matt Mason*, *Space
   Sled* and *Jet Pack*.

Accessories:

   A decal sheet was included in this
   set for the *Space Station*, *Space
   Crawler* and *Space Sled*.

Packaging:

   Boxed item - 25" x 14" x 9".

Part 2 - *Major Matt Mason:* Mattel's *Man In Space*

Stock Number: 6311
Item Name: *Space Crawler Action Set*
Copyright Date: 1966
Contents:

   This *Action Set* was a boxed item and came with *Major Matt Mason* with his white *Space Sled*, *Space Crawler* and *Jet Propulsion Pack*. Refer to the single items for further descriptions.

Accessories:

   Decal sheets were included in this set for the *Space Crawler*.

Packaging:

   Boxed item - 14¼" x 14¼" x 9½".

Stock Number: 3616
Item Name: *Major Matt Mason Space Ship Case*
Copyright Date: 1966
Contents:

   This large, foot and a half high rocket ship case was manufactured to "hold and store *Major Matt Mason* and his space equipment". It featured "two level full color interior, 3-D molded plastic contour couch and fold-down ramp". Standard Plastic Products Inc., A Mattel subsidiary, manufactured the carrying case.

Accessories:

   None.

Packaging:

   None. The Space Ship case was sold with a 3" x 4" yellow tag, depicting the case with ramp lowered, showing the interior of the case including blue removable plastic launch couch and clear plastic storage area on the lower level.

Part 2 - *Major Matt Mason*: Mattel's *Man In Space*

Stock Number: 3617
Item Name: *Sgt. Storm Flight Pak*
Copyright Date: 1967
Contents:

Sgt. Storm was sold with either his *Flight Pak* set or with his *Cat Trac* only. *Sgt. Storm* was introduced in the second year of production and was the second of four astronauts produced. He was actually a revised *Major Matt Mason* figure, in this incarnation wearing a reddish orange painted space suit and having a different molded head attached to an otherwise *Matt Mason* body. The *Flight Pak* contained the same accessories as the formerly listed *Major Matt Mason Flight Pak*, that being the *Sgt. Storm* figure, helmet, two-piece *Space Sled* and *Jet Propulsion Pak* plus *Space Sled* decal sheet.

Packaging:

Bubble blister card - 10" X 13".

Stock Number: 6318
Item Name: *Major Matt Mason with Cat Trac*
Copyright Date: 1967
Contents:

Major Matt Mason wearing his helmet was packaged sitting atop a red *Cat Trac* waving out of his square window box. The box artwork depicted a lunarscape with shadowed craters and cliff in the background.

Packaging:

Square Bubble Card - 5" x 8".

Part 2 - *Major Matt Mason: Mattel's Man In Space*

Stock Number: 6319
Item Name: **Sgt. Storm with Cat Trac**
Copyright Date: 1967
Contents:
   Sgt. Storm wearing his helmet was packaged sitting atop his white *Cat Trac*. He, as with *Major Matt*, was presented in a square window box. The box artwork was a colorful lunarscape. Unlike the *Matt Mason* card, which was trimmed with a black border, this card was trimmed in green.
Accessories:
   None.
Packaging:
   Square Bubble Card - 5" x 8".

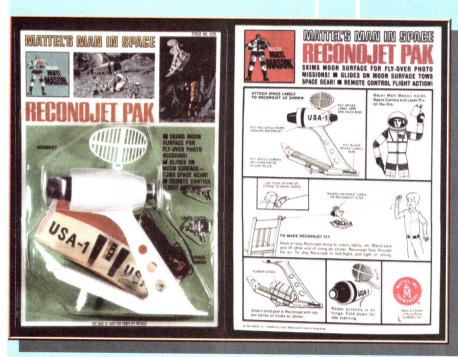

Stock Number: 6320
Item Name: **Reconojet Pak**
Copyright Date: 1967
Contents:
   The *Reconojet* was comprised of a white molded vehicle with a rotating radar dish. It included a black string with a red hook, and pull action moved it across the string length.
Accessories:
   A chromed space-type camera, laser gun and decal sheet.
Packaging:
   Bubble blister card - 8½" x 12".

Decals for #6320 *Reconojet Pak*

Part 2 - *Major Matt Mason: Mattel's Man In Space*

Stock Number: 6321
Item Name: *Space Shelter Pak*
Copyright Date: 1967
Contents:

This Mattel pak included a gray / silver inflator pump and a one-man blue tent with white graphics. The pump and tent were fitted into a backpack for the *Major*.

Accessories:

A paper map, white map case, and a compass. The compass included a small decal printed in yellow with a black-dialed face.

Packaging:

Bubble blister card - 8½" x 12".

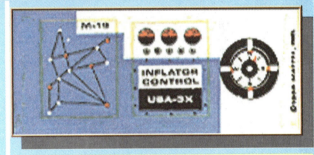

Decals for #6321 *Space Shelter Pak*

Stock Number: 6322
Item Name: *Satellite Locker*
Copyright Date: 1967
Contents:

This was a storage locker for *Major Matt*. It included colorful graphics similar to those found on other boxed and carded items. It had a number of compartments to hold not only the *Major*, but his space buddies as well. The exterior of the case was red vinyl with the interior a thin blue, easily broken vacuum-formed plastic.

Accessories:

A full size image of *Major Matt Mason* on a card was included in the window display area.

Packaging:

None. This item, similar to the *Space Ship Case*, was sold with a tag attached to the handle. It displayed a graphic of the toy showing equipment that could be stored within it.

Part 2 - *Major Matt Mason: Mattel's Man In Space*

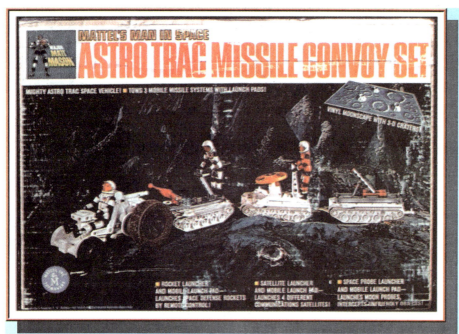

Stock Number: 6327
Item Name: *Astro Trac Missile Convoy Set*
Copyright Date: 1967
Contents:

This toy was sold only through SEARS. It contained the *Astro Trac* and three *Launch Platforms* made from white molded plastic. The platforms had their details molded into them, such as the tracks and wheels. They also came with small wheels which were attached on spindles that were located under the platforms. Also included in this large boxed set were three vacuum-formed moon craters and a light blue with dark blue / black detailed moonscape. The craters had snaps in the center which snapped to designated areas on the moonscape.

Accessories:

A *Satellite Launcher*, *Space Probe Launcher*, *Rocket Launcher*, *Rotojet Gun*, *Knife*, *sheath* and *belt*, two *walkie-talkies*, *decontamination gun* and *tank*, *binoculars*, and *flare gun*.

Packaging:

Boxed item.

Stock Number: 6328
Item Name: *Mobile Launch Pad*
Copyright Date: 1967
Contents:

This item was sold through SEARS and was the same item as included in the above *Astro Trac Missile Convoy Set*. It consisted of the same white molded platform, which could hold the *Space Probe Launcher*, *Rocket Launcher*, *Satellite Launcher* and *Gamma-Ray Gard* gun.

Accessories:

None.

Packaging:

Bubble blister card - 8½" x 12".

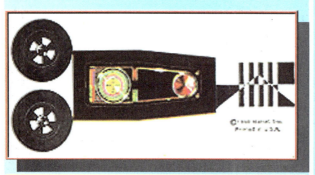

Decals for #6331 *Callisto* (opposite page)

Part 2 - *Major Matt Mason: Mattel's Man In Space*

Stock Number: 6330
Item Name: *Captain Laser*
Copyright Date: 1967
Contents:

This toy was billed as "*Major Matt Mason's* friend from Outer Space, Super human *Captain Lazer* was charged with astonishing lazer powers". He was a large (12") dark blue figure with silver molded boots, backpack, gloves, belt and gun. He came with an attached battery / back, which allowed his accessories to flash. He displayed "flashing eyes, chest beams and solar buzz".

Accessories:

Radiation Shield, Lazer Wand, Cosmic Beacon, Flashing Lazer Beacon, Space Tredder boots and silver space helmet.

Packaging:

Boxed item - 14¾" x 10" x 5" window box with blue and black graphics.

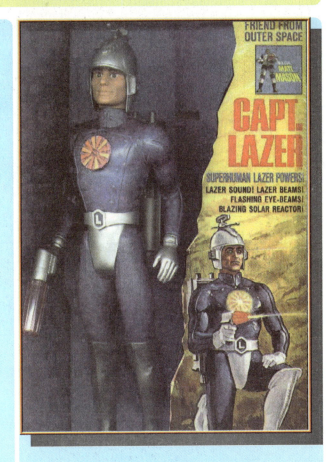

Stock Number: 6331
Item Name: *Callisto*
Copyright Date: 1968
Contents:

Callisto was the "mysterious alien from Jupiter." He stood 6" tall and was a rubber reinforced "bendie" like his space explorer friend *Matt Mason*. He was molded in black rubber accessory type legs and arms. His suit was a dark painted green with blue accents and his green molded head was transparent. Face detailing included white skull lines, white eyes with red and black pupils, bushy black eyebrows, and white lips. *Callisto* came with light green boots with blue trim and green hands with similar blue trim at the cuffs.

Accessories:

Purple shoulder harness with attached backpack and snap on *Laser Sensor* with yellow line. This item came with a purple air pump and clear tubing to allow the sensor to snap in and out. Decals were included with this figure for detailing the removable shoulder space sensor equipment.

Packaging:

Bubble blister card - 8¹/₁₆" x 8¹/₁₆".

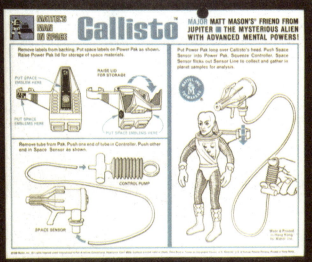

Part 2 - *Major Matt Mason*: Mattel's *Man In Space*

Stock Number: 6332
Item Name: *Jeff Long - Space Scientist Rocketry*

Copyright Date: 1968
Contents:
   Jeff Long was the black American astronaut produced for the Mattel's *Major Matt Mason* line of toys. He was molded in black with painted blue suit, black strap details and white pockets.

Accessories:
   White helmet with yellow visor, and white *CAT Trac*.

Packaging:
   Squared Bubble Card - 5" x 8". The graphic on the card includes the Lunar Module descending to the moon surface. The card has an orange background.

Stock Number: 6333
Item Name: *Doug Davis Space Scientist Radiologist - with CAT Trac*

Copyright Date: 1968
Contents:
   Doug Davis comes in a yellow space suit. He has black strapping with a white zipper. He is displayed sitting on his red *CAT Trac*.

Accessories:
   White helmet with yellow visor, and red *CAT Trac*.

Packaging:
   Squared Bubble Card - 5" x 8". The graphic on card includes a moonscape with space station with green highlights.

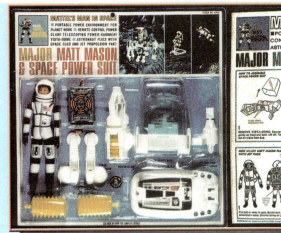

Stock Number: 6336
Item Name: *Major Matt Mason and Space Power Suit*
Copyright Date: 1968
Contents:

Similar to the *Major Matt Mason Moon Suit Pack*, this item includes a *Matt Mason*, white helmet with yellow visor, two yellow bellows to operate the *Space Power Suit*, *Power Suit* dark blue dome and white base, clear tubing, two piece *Space Sled*, *Jet Propulsion* unit and two space boot attachments.

Accessories:
Decal sheets are included with this item.

Packaging:
Bubble blister card - 13" x 14".

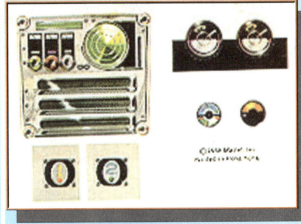

Decals for #6336 *Major Matt Mason and Space Power Suit*

Stock Number: 6337
Item Name: *Space Mission Team*
Copyright Date: 1968
Contents:

This set came in a photo box displaying the figures of *Major Matt Mason* standing on the lunar surface, *Callisto* wearing his sensor shoulder harness, *Sgt. Storm* skimming over the moon's surface on his *Space Sled* and *Doug Davis* driving his red *Cat Trac*. The box is titled "Four Expert Astronauts Equipped for Planet Travel and Exploration.

Accessories:
A decal sheet was included for the *Space Sled* with this boxed set.

Packaging:
Boxed item.

Part 2 - *Major Matt Mason: Mattel's Man In Space*

Decals for #6340 *Firebolt Space Cannon*

Stock Number: 6339
Item Name: **Uni-Tred and Space Bubble**
Copyright Date: 1968
Contents:

Two D-size batteries powered this item. The large box came with a front graphic displaying the red *Uni-Tred* pulling the *Space Bubble* up a lunar mountain. *Matt Mason* was operating the Uni-Tred, while *Sgt. Storm* rode in the *Space Bubble*. The *Uni-Tred* was made up of the red chassis, white inner frame and black treaded mechanism. Included was a white two-piece tow-yoke. The *Bubble* included a "gyro-seat" that kept the astronaut upright while traversing the lunar surface.

Accessories:

Decals for both the *Uni-Tred* and the *Space Bubble* were included with this set.

Packaging:

Large colorful box with litho applied to face, and blue and black line graphics on other box sides.

Stock Number: 6340
Item Name: **Firebolt Space Cannon**
Copyright Date: 1967
Contents:

This box included the *Space Cannon*, a large battery operated toy with both lights and sound. The barrel pulsed a bright red color when the *Space Cannon*'s lever was switched on, allowing the turret to rotate with the large black wheels propelling this vehicle forward. The radar screen should light up.

Accessories:

A decal sheet was included with this item.

Packaging:

Small boxed set - 16" x 8" x 12".

Part 2 - *Major Matt Mason: Mattel's Man In Space*

Stock Number: 6341

Item Name: *Firebolt Space Cannon Super Action Set*

Copyright Date: 1967

Contents:

This set came in a large picture box with figures of *Major Matt Mason*, *Sgt. Storm*, and *Captain Lazer* sold together with the *Firebolt Space Cannon*.

Accessories:

Cat Trac and *Jet Propulsion Pak*, and decals for the *Firebolt Space Cannon*.

Packaging:

Large graphically rich box showing a frontal face graphic of *Captain Lazer* piloting the *Cannon* over the lunar surface. *Major Matt Mason* is shown operating his *Cat Trac*, while *Sgt. Storm* flies overhead.

Decals for #6343 *Supernaut Power Limbs Pak*

Stock Number: 6342

Item Name: *Gamma Ray-Gard Pak*

Copyright Date: 1968

Contents:

This missile firing turret sitting on its own red three-legged pedestal consisted of a two piece design — the pedestal and the gun-type turret.

Accessories:

Included in this pack were four missiles. Decals were also included to enhance the *Gamma Ray Gard* missile firing defense system.

Packaging:

Bubble blister card - 8½" x 12".

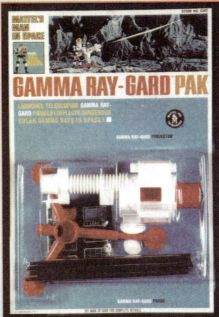

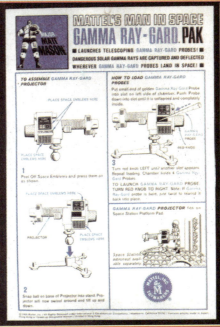

Stock Number: 6343

Item Name: *Supernaut Power Limbs Pak*

Copyright Date: 1968

Contents:

This yellow plastic apparatus held one astronaut at a time. It was able to extend both the legs and claw-like arms. This toy came with molded-in backpack and functional claws.

Accessories:

A small hook is included on the rear of the *Power Limbs*. A decal sheet was also included on the card.

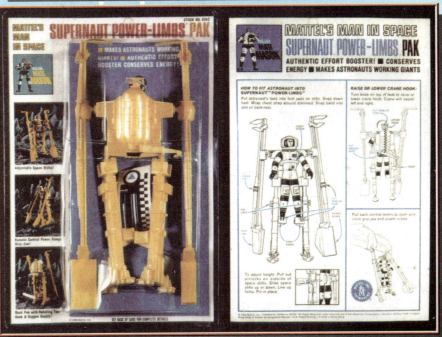

Packaging:

Bubble blister card - 8½" x 12".

Part 2 - Major Matt Mason: Mattel's *Man In Space*

Accessories:

This set comprised a molded base, "power hammer", "power claw", blue "vista-dome", two yellow bellows, tubing, and white molded plastic attachments that *Matt*'s feet fit into to provide stability. A small decal sheet was included with this item.

Packaging:

Bubble blister card - 8½" X 12".

Stock Number: 6344
Item Name: ***Space Power Suit Pak***
Copyright Date: 1968
Contents:

The *Power Suit Pak* is an environmental suit to protect *Major Matt Mason* and his space buddies from the hazards of interstellar space. It consisted of a white base with molded interior console. Attached to each side of the base were two mechanisms, one a bellow operated claw and on the other side a bellow operated "telescoping power hammer". A blue dome protected *Matt Mason*, who was sold separately.

Stock Number: 6345
Item Name: ***Space Bubble***
Copyright Date: 1968

Contents:

The *Space Bubble* is a 7" diameter ball with a gyro-command seat placed in it. The seat remains level while the bubble rotates 360° as it is towed by any of a number of *Major Matt Mason* motorized vehicles. A white, molded two piece frame supports the bubble.

Accessories:

White molded "tow yoke" adapter unit and decal sheet.

Packaging:

Small box - 9½" x 10¾" x 7½". The box art included graphics of the *Space Bubble* being towed by the *Space Crawler* across the lunar surface.

Part 2 - *Major Matt Mason:* Mattel's *Man In Space*

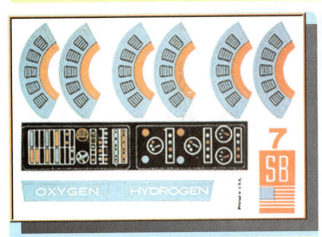

Decals for #6345 *Space Bubble* (previous page)

Decals for #6346 *Uni-Tred Space Hauler*

Stock Number: 6346
Item Name: **Uni-Tred Space Hauler**
Copyright Date: 1968
Contents:

The *Uni-Tred* was sold not only in the sets listed (# 6339, #6353), but also as a single boxed item. This red molded plastic vehicle could climb just about any mountain terrain and towed the *Space Bubble*. It operated on two D-size batteries. The *Uni-Tred* was actually made of three separate parts — the body wide tread, the white molded frame and the red molded chassis.

Accessories:

The *Uni-Tred* came with a decal sheet.

Packaging:

This item came in a small box similar in size to the *Space Bubble*.

Stock Number: 6347
Item Name: *Space Travel Pak*
Copyright Date: 1968
Contents:

This carded pack came with a number of space equipment items to make *Major Matt's* working in space easier. Included on the card were the *Space Propulsion Pak*, silver decontamination rifle including yellow tanks, blue belt and black hose and a two piece *Space Sled*.

Accessories:

This *Travel Pak* came with a decal sheet to be applied to the *Space Sled*.

Packaging:

Blister bubble card - 8½" x 12".

Part 2 - *Major Matt Mason*: Mattel's *Man In Space*

Stock Number: 6351
Item Name: ***Firebolt Space Cannon Action Set with Captain Lazer***
Copyright Date: 1968
Contents:

The *Firebolt Space Cannon Action Set* included not only the *Space Cannon*, but also the *Captain Lazer* figure. Both items were sold separately in the above mentioned *Captain Lazer* box (#6330) and the *Firebolt*

Space Cannon box (#6340.)
Accessories:

Included boxed with this item was a decal sheet for the *Space Cannon* and "helmet, *Paralyzer Wand, Radiation Shield* and *Space Tredder* boots."
Packaging:

The *Firebolt Space Cannon Action Set with Captain Lazer* came in a large litho box with colorful graphics on the front face depicting the *Captain* with his *Cannon*.

Stock Number: 6353
Item Name: ***Lunar Base Command Set***
Copyright Date: 1968
Contents:

The *Lunar Base Command Set* is the largest box set in the Mattel's *Man in Space* series of toys. Included in this box set were the *Space Station* (#6308), *Space Bubble* (#6345), *Uni-Tred* (#6346), *Space Crawler* (#6304), *Major Matt Mason Flight Pak* (#6300), and *Callisto* (#6331.)
Accessories:

This set came with all accompanying decal sheets that were sold separately with each toy. *Major Matt Mason* and *Callisto* came with their cards and accessories.
Packaging:

The bendie figures were included on blister cards in this set.

Stock Number: 6355
Item Name: ***Space Discovery Set***
Copyright Date: 1968
Contents:

The *Space Discovery Set* includes items that were also sold separately, but were now repackaged in a good looking litho boxed set. *Callisto*, astronaut *Doug Davis* with his *Cat Trac*, the *Space Crawler, Space Bubble* and *Space Power Suit* (#'s 6331, 6333, 6304, 6345, and 6344) came individually carded or boxed along with their respective decal sheets.
Accessories:

Doug Davis came on a card with his *Cat Trac*, as did *Callisto* with his space sensor equipment.

Part 2 - *Major Matt Mason:* **Mattel's** *Man In Space*

Packaging:

A large, graphic rich box of a moonscape with mountains. Steam rises from a crater as *Callisto* pilots the *Space Crawler* and *Bubble* across the lunar surface. *Doug Davis* operates inside a *Space Power Suit* to the left.

Stock Number: 6356
Item Name: *Orbitor with Or*
Notes:

This toy was advertised in the 1970 Mattel dealer catalogue, but there is no evidence that it was developed beyond the prototype stage. The only picture that I've seen of this figure and his saucer ship is from the Mattel catalogue. The promo literature reads "*Or* was a strange shaped blue colored visitor from Orion with a yellow 12" Frisbee or rotor like space craft with a clear dome or canopy that was launched with the pull of a power cord attached to a special impact plastic and steel launcher. Up...up it soars, whirling toward a space adventure!".

Stock Number: 6357
Item Name: *Star Seeker with Memory Guidance System*
Copyright Date: 1969
Contents:

The *Star Seeker* capsule is a white space ship operated by a D-size battery. It included 11 orange pegs which, when fit into the blue console base, programmed a multitude of directional moves. When placed on the floor, the ship would run along by means of three small rubber wheels. The cockpit of the ship, which was located on the top, had a flip up blue "vista dome" which held one of the *Major Matt Mason* figures or *Callisto*. *Captain Lazer* wouldn't fit in this capsule, nor would *Scorpio*.

Accessories:

A decal sheet was included with this toy. Also included with this item were planet cutouts of our solar system.

Packaging:

The *Star Seeker with Memory Guidance System* was sold in a hexagonal 12" high box. Box graphics were in shades of blue and purple, highlighted by an artist's rendition of *Major Matt Mason* sitting at the controls of the *Star Seeker*.

Part 2 - *Major Matt Mason*: Mattel's Man In Space

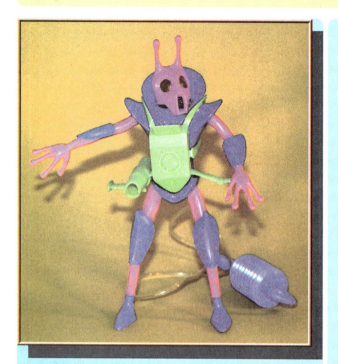

Stock Number: 6359
Item Name: *Scorpio*
Copyright Date: 1969
Contents:

    Scorpio was the final figure marketed by Mattel. He was battery operated and stood several inches over the *Matt Mason* figures. He was manufactured with a removable head (where the battery was placed.) *Scorpio* had "bendie" pink molded arms, legs and head. He came with purple hard plastic feet and a torso with integrated shoulders and collar.

Accessories:

    Scorpio had a number of accessories made of hard plastic, including two purple shin guards, two purple elbow guards, lime green chest projector that fired white Styrofoam "*search globes*", clear tubing and purple bellows.

Packaging:

    Boxed item - 8" x 13" x 2". *Scorpio* is displayed behind a celo window and can be seen wearing his shin and elbow guards. The box art includes an artist's rendition of *Scorpio* drawn from a side / front profile.

Stock Number: 6360
Item Name: *XRG-1 Re-entry Glider*
Copyright Date: 1968
Contents:

    This *Glider* was the equivalent of the NASA space shuttle for *Major Matt Mason*, his buddies and *Callisto*. The *Glider*, which had a wing span of 18", was manufactured in white vacuum-formed plastic. It had a detachable canopy.

Accessories:

    The *Glider* was sold with a decal sheet of the console, an American flag, and *XRG-1* labels. The black and orange labeling on the *XRG-1* was installed at the point of manufacture.

Packaging:

    This was the largest carded Mattel *Major Matt Mason: Man In Space* item (18½" x 21⅝" x 4⅝". The card was richly colored with graphics of all the action figures, less *Scorpio* and *Captain Lazer*, on the upper right corner.

Decals for #6360 *XRG-1 Re-entry Glider*

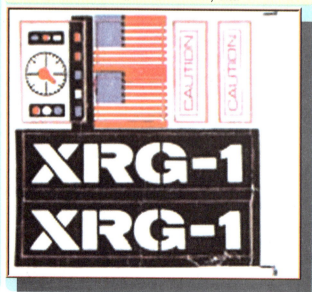

Part 2 - *Major Matt Mason: Mattel's Man In Space*

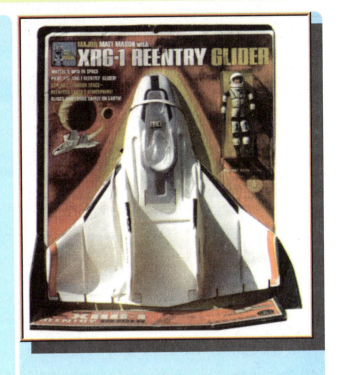

Stock Number: 6361
Item Name: **XRG-1 Reentry Glider with Major Matt Mason**
Copyright Date: 1968
Contents:
   This *Major Matt Mason* toy includes the same *Re-entry Glider* as item #6360. This item also included a *Major Matt Mason* figure.
Accessories:
   This set included *Major Matt Mason* and a decal sheet as in #6360.
Packaging:
   With the exception of *Major Matt Mason* held on a bubble on the upper most left of the large card and new card art colors, this item was similar to #6360.

Stock Number: 6362
Item Name: *Talking Major Matt Mason*
Copyright Date: 1969
Contents:
   The *Talking Major Matt Mason* pack came with the white *Major Matt* figure plus the *Talking Backpack*. The *Backpack* was a re-mold of the original, but slightly larger in size. The talking box inside the toy was programmed to make five different statements as the black cord was pulled from the top of the toy.
Accessories:
   Major Matt's helmet and visor, decals and instructions.
Packaging:
   This item came in a square box 10" x 3¾" x 7½" with illustrations of the *Major* flying with the use of his pack. The illustrated box art was similar to that of the *Star Seeker* box artwork.

Part 2 - *Major Matt Mason:* Mattel's *Man In Space*

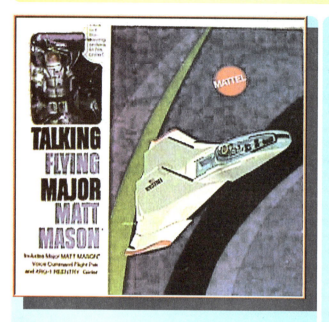

Stock Number: 6378
Item Name: **Talking Major Matt Mason with XRG-1 Reentry Glider**
Copyright Date: 1969
Contents:

This pack included number 6362 (*Major Matt Mason* with *Talking Back Pack*) and the *Re-entry Glider*. This is a large closed box set which included graphics of the *Major* flying his *Glider*. *Major Matt Mason* could be seen at the top left of the box wearing his *Talking Backpack*. This toy was advertised as a "superb combination value" by Mattel, and is now, many years later, one of the most expensive and elusive *Matt* combination items.

Accessories:

Decal sheets were included for the *Glider* as in #6360.

Packaging:

Large colorfully illustrated closed box. The box art depicted an illustration of the *Glider* in flight with shades of blue bands behind it.

Stock Number: 6379
Item Name: **Major Matt Mason Super Power Equipment Set**
Copyright Date: 1969
Contents:

This set came with items previously packaged in other *Matt Mason* sets. Included together in this "Super Set" was *Major Matt Mason*, the *Power Limbs* and the *Space Power Suit*.

Accessories:

This set also included a red *Cat Trac* and decal sets for the *Space Power Suit* and *Power Limbs*, plus a white *Major Matt Mason* figure, helmet and visor.

Packaging:

This brightly illustrated box in shades of pink is striking. The box art includes renditions of the *Major* using both the *Power Limbs* and the *Power Suit*. At the lower left of the box is a cut out celo window. From behind this cutout, *Major Matt* can be seen affixed to his red *Cat Trac* waving to the prospective buyer.

Stock Number: 6380
Item Name: **Voyage to Galaxy III Set**
Notes:

As with *Or* and his saucer the *Orbitor*, the *Voyage to Galaxy III* Mattel *Man in Space Playset* is not believed to exist. It appears to have been planned by Mattel, but, perhaps due to waning interest in the toy lineup, was never produced.

Stock Number: 6386
Item Name: ***Star Seeker Walk in Space Set***
Copyright Date: 1969
Contents:

This boxed set included the above mentioned *Star Seeker* and a *Major Matt Mason* figure. This set was unique in that it included, for the first, time a thin black wire that supported *Major Matt* so that he appeared to space walk outside of the *Star Seeker*. An orange tube was included with this set which represented a "lifeline" from the *Major* to the *Star Seeker*.

Accessories:

Major Matt Mason, helmet, visor, wiring, orange tubing, decal sheet.

Packaging:

Similar to other late *Major Matt Mason* box artwork, this box also included brightly illustrated artist's renditions of the *Major* floating free outside of his capsule. Illustrations of the capsule alone were copies of the illustrations utilized on item #6357 (*Star Seeker*.) Unlike #6357, that came in a hexagon box, this item was sold in a square box.

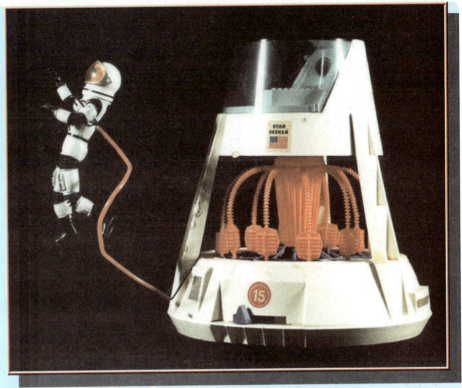

Stock Number: 8178
Item Name: ***Astro Trac Gift Set***
Contents:

I'd like to thank Mr. Larry Chinn, who provided this information on the previously unknown *Astro Trac Gift Set*. This set came with a Mobile Launcher, *Astro Trac*, *Satellite Launch Pak*, *Sgt. Storm* and *Major Matt Mason*. This item was sold through the SEARS outlets in Canada only and was not issued in the United States.

Packaging:

The box was similar in size to the packaged *Astro Trac* box. It was printed in the basic blue, black and white printing with line illustrations on all sides.

Part 2 - *Major Matt Mason: Mattel's Man In Space*

Stock Number: 8874
Item Name: *Astronaut - Generic box*
Contents:

Major Matt Mason, Sgt. Storm, Doug Davis and *Jeff Long* were each sold as individual items through various Space Administrations including Cape Canaveral in Cocoa Beach, Florida. I personally recall all of the astronauts being sold in small generic boxes on one of my many Christmas vacation trips as a child to NASA and Fort Lauderdale. A special note of thanks goes to my parent who finally gave in and bought me that blue astronaut patched flight suit that I begged for.

Packaging:

The smallish 7" x 2" box held only one of the four astronauts. The boxes were a white mailer type with clear see-through box lids. Each box simply stated "Astronaut with bendable spacesuit" on the bottom of the box. There was no designation for which *Major Matt Mason* bendie figure was in the box, and they were not called *Major Matt Mason* toys or identified as being manufactured by Mattel toys. These boxed figures appeared late in the production life of this toy series.

Major Matt Mason And His Space Buddies

Sgt. Storm - Matt Mason's high spirited partner

Major Matt Mason was the first "bendie" released for Mattel's *Man in Space* toy line in 1967. Mattel's design team utilized the Mercury astronauts' space suits as the design theme for this toy. Through his almost four-year production run, *Matt Mason* was redesigned and refined to correct initial quality difficulties. *Matt Mason* was a "bendie", and as such, was manufactured from a pliable rubber compound molded over a wire skeletal frame.

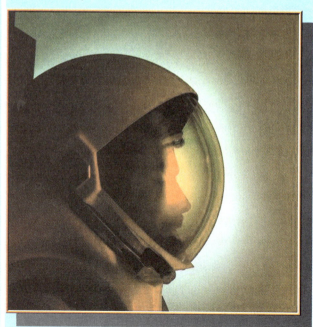

NASA concept helmet on which Mattel based *Man In Space* toys

Part 2 - *Major Matt Mason*: Mattel's *Man In Space*

The white molded figure was soon discontinued because of quality problems. It was found that the black paint used for the "accordion" arm and leg joints didn't hold up well under children's play.

On Christmas morning 1967, *Major Matt Mason* and his *Space Station* were found sitting under many a young boy's Christmas tree. He became an icon heralding the new era of the Space Race, along with his "high spirited partner" *Sgt. Storm*, "Space Scientist - Radiologist" *Doug Davis*, and "Scientist and Rocketry expert" *Jeff Long*.

Mattel's *Man in Space* line of toys was to become one of the best remembered boy's toys of the late 1960's. Around the world little boys dreamed of becoming Mercury and Gemini astronauts and *Major Matt Mason* helped them live out these fanciful dreams. Mattel, capitalizing on the race to the moon, created an elaborate series of toys, for the first year based on "real" NASA designs. During the second, third and fourth years, toy design became even more elaborate, but also less scientifically accurate, with more of an emphasis on science fiction. *Major Matt Mason* was the first astronaut released in 1967. The design for the *Major* was loosely based on the Mercury astronaut space suit design. His space buddies *Sgt. Storm*, *Doug Davis* and *Jeff Long* (who was the only African-American in the group) joined him in the second year of production. These "bendie" figures were made of rubberized plastic molded over a metal skeletal frame. They had wonderful play value since they could be bent in almost any position and were highly poseable. Unfortunately, the metal wiring was very fine and frequently snapped. This would render the figure more or less unposeable. The bendie space suited figures were initially highly detailed.

During the almost four years that production of the line continued in North America, detailing became less intricate. The *Man in Space* astronauts came with some very cool and authentic looking white "plastiformed" helmets with moveable yellow tinted visors. All the space vehicles designed for the *Man in Space* series of toys fit all four astronauts. In 1968 *Major Matt Mason's* "friend from Mars, *Captain Lazer*" joined the toy lineup.

The *Captain* was made of hard plastic and was jointed. He towered over the 6" "bendies" at 12" in height. The 1969 Mattel catalogue stated that he was an "amazing superhuman spaceman" who "sends sonar sound waves from his Solar Reactor when his battery-operated power pack is activated from his Cosmic Coder." He had "flashing eye beams" and "powerful solar chest reactor." Because of his enormous height, he fit only one vehicle in the *Man in Space* toy line, the *Firebolt Space Cannon*. It's not clear why he was included in the

An artist's rendering of *Matt Mason's* space suit on a lunar background

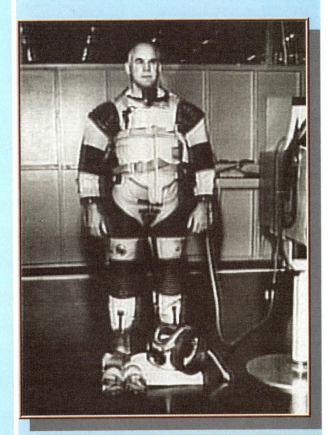

Prototype Gemini space suit on which *Matt Mason* suits were based

Part 2 - *Major Matt Mason*: Mattel's *Man In Space*

Space Scientist - Radiologist *Doug Davis*

Scientist and Rocketry expert *Jeff Long*

line of toys. It's been proposed that he may have been designed for another line of toys. Another theory is that he may have been included to appeal to owners of the popular *G.I Joe* large series of boy's toys.

In 1969 the *Space Mission Team* was joined by *Callisto*, the "mysterious astronaut from Jupiter." This "amazing alien joined *Major Matt Mason's* space explorers". He looked evil and wicked and I, as did many other boys, made him an enemy, when in fact he was described as an "alien friend" in the literature. *Callisto* came with a "transparent skull which revealed a highly developed humanoid brain endowed with superior mental powers." He was manufactured using the same process as the "bendie" astronauts — a rubberized plastic, molded over a metal skeletal frame. The spring (1969) Mattel vendor's catalogue described *Callisto's* accessory as a "removable shoulder-mounted *Space Sensor*." It functioned by releasing a "retractable *Sensor Line* for sampling unknown space matter." It operated by way of

a "coil-action *Space Sensor* and "remote control" air bellow which was made of purple molded plastic.

In 1970, late in the life of these toys, the rare and elusive *Scorpio* was manufactured. He is rare since he was shipped separately, in limited quantities at best. He was also made in the final year, as opposed to *Major Matt Mason* who was manufactured to the end of production, almost a full four years. *Scorpio* was *Major Matt Mason's* "mysterious ally from the stars with flashing electronic eyes! Bendable arms and legs, hundreds of action poses". He stood a full 8" tall, two more than *Matt Mason*, his "bendie" buddies and *Callisto*. *Scorpio* was battery operated. One AA-size battery made his eyes and mouth flash. He was a very 1970's hot pink color wearing purple body armor with arm and shin guards. *Scorpio* was sold with a lime green colored harness which shot Styrofoam "search globes". The harness combination chest pack was operated by a purple bellow. The story of *Scorpio* (reprinted from the

Part 2 - *Major Matt Mason*: Mattel's *Man In Space*

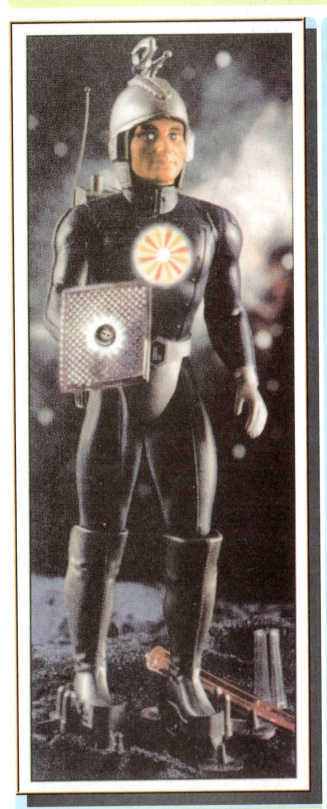

Major Matt Mason's friend from Mars, Captain Lazer

Callisto, Matt Mason's alien friend from Jupiter

Scorpio, Major Matt Mason's mysterious ally from the stars

packing box) states that:

"*Scorpio*'s cocoon snapped open and he tumbled onto the dry sands of his planet in the star cluster Scorpio. Although *Scorpio* would never know his parents as

Earth children would, he was prepared to face anything from the moment of birth. His keen mind could sense danger before it appeared. The strange electronic cells

Part 2 - *Major Matt Mason:* Mattel's *Man In Space*

in his brain were programmed like computers. All the information he required came instantly. He opened his eyes and they began to flash. He realized he could read minds. Suddenly a sharp sound-thought screamed into his brain. It was a call from a far-away galaxy. *Scorpio's* next sensation was the soft kiss of stardust, the whisper of space, as he blasted out and away from his home. The new planet where *Scorpio* landed was totally unexplored. Strangely, though, he could sense another presence. Quickly he strapped on his vest projector. But before he could gather his search globes, he saw the alien. It was *Major Matt Mason*. *Scorpio's* senses told him that this was the creature that had called him. This must be a friend. Without a word, *Scorpio* turned and followed *Major Matt Mason* into a world of adventure".

Major Matt Mason And His Spaced-Out Vehicles

This chapter will explore both the mechanical and non-mechanical operation of all of Mattel's *Man in Space* toys. Often times, *Major Matt Mason* vehicles and accessories are found unboxed. This being the case, instructions are most often missing. I will attempt to describe the action that the ship or vehicle was designed for and also discuss its mechanical operation. Mattel was a highly inventive company and Mattel's *Man in Space* line of toys remains today as one of the most imaginative and inventive toys from the 1960's. The popularity of this toy line can be linked not only to the fervor created by the U.S. quest to land the first man on the moon, but also to the realism and durability of the toys themselves. Many of the original designs were based on NASA schematics, and Mattel's savvy marketing department used this to enhance the play value of this line-up. Not only did John Glenn orbit the earth, but also thanks to Mattel, every little boy could experience the same thrill in his living room with *Major Matt* and all his "real" accessories.

The Non-Mechanical Toys:

Cat Trac / Lunar Trac
The *Man in Space* line-up of toys began with the most common item found today — the *Cat Trac*, or *Lunar Trac* as it is named on some box artwork. It was really just a lump of white or red molded plastic, but, to a little boy of nine years of age, it was the space vehicle of choice. The *Cat Trac*, with its molded treads and seven wheels, could carry *Matt* through any kind of alien terrain. With seating capacity for only one and steering by way of two molded shifters located on the console, *Matt's* feet were firmly locked in the boot housings so that he could explore alien worlds. Many a bendie astronaut was sold on the blister card sitting atop either the white or red *Cat Trac*, waving out of his window box to the prospective little astronaut begging his mother to buy him. The box artwork sets the stage stating that

"Mattel's *Man in Space*, *Major Matt Mason* roams the dark side of the moon on his one-man *Lunar Trac*."

Space Sled
The *Space Sled* was another accessory toy. Mattel stated this item was "special and enabled the Mattel astronauts to better explore the universe." It was "adapted from official space program designs", and "was completely safe and durable." The *Sled* was never sold as an individual item, but came in many *Paks* including *Major Matt Mason with Moon Suit* and the *Space Travel Pak*, as well as the boxed sets *The Space Station* and *Space Crawler Deluxe Action Set*. The *Major*, or one of his astronaut buddies, could stand on the platform base, locking in his heels, and hold on to the handle grips. Cutouts were designed into the base of the sled to attach the *Jet Propulsion Pak*. The *Space Sled* would then fly or glide over the surface of the moon, terrifying an alien city or your gold shag living room carpet. Pull the red knob from the top of the *Jet Pak* and watch the

The *Major* does patrol duty on his *Reconojet*

Part 2 - Major Matt Mason: Mattel's *Man In Space*

Jeff Long with the Mattel's *Space Sled*

Space Sled move with blazing speed. With the help of the *Major's Jet Pak*, the *Space Sled* could make its way to the "*Space Station* Moon headquarters, climbing lunar rocks and circling volcanic moon craters."

Reconojet
The *Reconojet* was an "aerial craft with remote control"

Matt Mason in his *Space Power Suit*

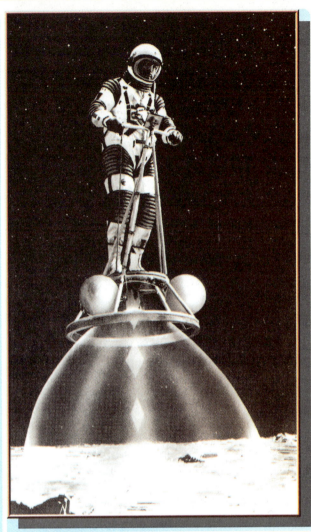

NASA design concept jet platform leading to the *Space Sled*

powered engine and platform that *Major Matt* could fly. The *Major* could be placed on the jet and, when the red hooked strings from either end of the turbine engine were attached to the legs of your mother's favorite table and chair, the *Reconojet* would whirl down its black string with spinning antenna and screeching sound. This created the most excitement for a non-mechanical toy. With what initially seemed like hundreds of feet of thin black string powering this vehicle, any giant lumbering alien or furry wildebeest, roaming through its flight path could be caught up in its black web. With what seemed like an endless supply of knots and kinks, this toy could be grounded for many hours. Over time the *Reconojet* often flew shorter and shorter distances thanks to the special astronaut's tool — scissors.

Space Power Suit
The *Space Power Suit* was an otherworldly "9 inch portable power environment." *Jeff Long, Sgt. Storm, Major Matt* or *Doug Davis* fit snugly inside the "blue vista dome" and control console, which provided fresh air for him while he protected earth and explored the

Part 2 - Major Matt Mason: Mattel's *Man In Space*

frigid cold reaches of outer space. With two yellow bellows, the "remote-control grasping power claw" and "telescoping power hammer" could be opened and closed. The huge powerful claw could mine the likes of Jupiter or the rings of Saturn. The big shoes, well, in reality, they just kept the *Major* from falling over as often. The special power boots, with a little imagination, would propel *Matt* through space faster than the speed of light or ski on the alien red planet Mars.

The *Moon Suit* was similar to the *Space Power Suit*, being bellow operated and air driven. This suit had flexible rubber arms, which were supposed to look like *Matt's* arms were inside them. He actually stood straight up inside the molded interior shell of the *Moon Suit*. The yellow bellows, when squeezed, forced air into the black pliable rubber arms and they sprang to life. Unfortunately, the soft rubber compounds for the arms are unstable and most have disintegrated over time. These arms are difficult to find in good shape, carded or otherwise.

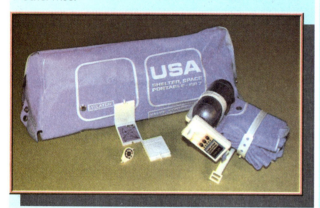

A lone astronaut's best friend is his *Space Shelter*

Space Shelter
The portable *Space Shelter* was yet another great toy for the *Major*. Matt Mason, or any of his astronaut buddies, was able to carry the tent and inflator pump using the white plastic travel harness. The harness also held a yellow faced non-functional compass to help the major explore alien terrain while looking for his evil arch villains, *Callisto* and *Scorpio*. The blue pup tent could be inflated by way of an inflator pump, which was a silver colored tank that attached to the backpack harness. The inflated tent enabled both *Major Matt* or one of his buddies to keep safe and warm, protected from red-hot meteors and exploding volcanoes, flowing lava beds or small streams in your backyard.

Power-Limbs
The stilts, or *Power Limbs* as Mattel called them, were brightly colored yellow arm and leg extensions. Once *Major Matt* was strapped into the "remote-control super boost equipment", he was almost invincible. With

Sgt. Storm out and about on his *Supernaut Power-Limbs*

the units' built in air tank and finger operated large claw and shovel, the limbs could be opened and closed by remote control. *Matt's Power Limbs* also had a hook and twist winch located at the rear of the unit. The legs of the *Power Limbs* could be raised and lowered by clips located in each leg. The major looked fierce operating this Mattel accessory, but keeping him standing straight was always a challenge. The *Power Limbs* offered a lesson in balancing, since, without careful positioning, the *Major* would teeter over crashing to the alien lunar surface.

Rocket Launcher, Space Probe and Satellite Launcher
Major Matt Mason could protect himself and the rest of his *Space Mission Team* from the alien attack of chloride

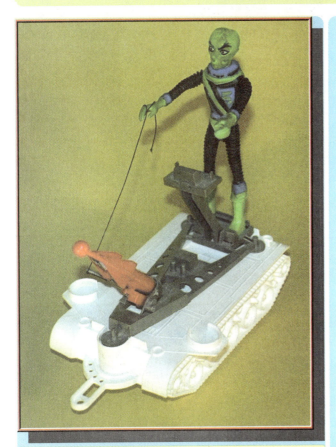

Callisto operates the *Space Probe* on the *Mobile Launch Pad*

breathing reptilian space creatures and communicate with the outer rim planets using his *Rocket Launcher*, *Space Probe* and *Satellite Launcher*. All three of these

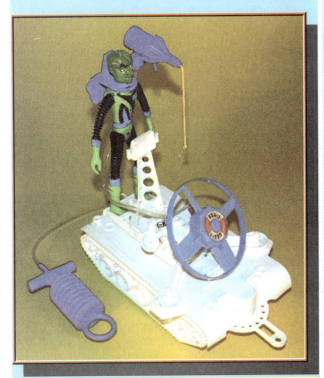

The *Satellite Launcher* ready to launch one of its three *Satellites*

accessory items were spring-loaded devices that could shoot projectiles. The *Rocket Launcher* and *Satellite Launcher* could shoot missile type projectiles, so watch out. Our house cat would run in terror as these two toys were taken out of the toy box. They could fly with such force that they could damage, if not disintegrate, the cowering space alien trapped in the corner. The three *Launchers* could be mounted onto the *Space Station*, *Mobile Launch Pad* or in the backyard sandbox. From these strategic positions, they could send back messages to the lunar base, communicate with earth or attack the giant furry other-worldly creature that continually attempted to investigate their crater potted mission control center when I wasn't looking.

PRICE

No. 6316

Major MATT MASON ™
SPACE SHIP CASE
by Mattel

Holds and stores Major Matt Mason and space equipment

- two level full color interior!
- 3-D molded plastic contour couch
- fold-down ramp!

© 1966 Mattel, Inc.

(see back for details)   doll not included

Spaceship Carrying Case

While not really a toy in the truest meaning, this *Rocket Ship Carrying Case* stood more than 18" tall. This was *Major Matt Mason's* home away from home. It was made of vinyl and was highly detailed. The *Ship* could be launched while *Matt* rested on his launch couch enroute to his latest adventure. Since the rocket was very large, it would easily accommodate all of *Matt's* buddies, and his alien friends too. Entrance and exit to this graphically detailed ship was made easy by way of a large fold down ramp, even his *Cat Trac* and space gear could be packed for "away missions."

Part 2 - *Major Matt Mason: Mattel's Man In Space*

Major Matt in his *Moon Suit* sporting chromed tool accessories

The multipurpose *Mobile Launch Pad*

Moon Suit Pak

The moon suit was one of the first year items available for the *Major Matt Mason* line of toys. The *Moon Suit* was based on NASA designs and a very similar design of the "real" NASA suit, which graced the cover of LIFE MAGAZINE in 1969. Mattel boxed artwork stated that the suit "must be worn when moon walking ... protects astronaut from solar radiation and meteorites, extreme heat and cold ... and has remote control arms." The suit consisted of two white plastic molded pieces that fit around any of the astronaut action figures. The *Major* could view the world through his clear suit face glass. The most impressive aspect of this suit, however, was the clever bellow operated arms. *Matt* appeared to come to life as the black rubberized arms stretched out and retracted when the air actuated yellow bellow was squeezed pumping air into the empty moon suit arms. Today, some thirty years after the first *Moon Suit* pack was manufactured, it's difficult to almost impossible to locate this toy with functional arms. The rubber, in most cases, dries out over time, becoming brittle. This suit came with three accessories including a hammer, screwdriver and wrench, and radiation detector, which fit onto the suit outer shell.

Mobile Launch Pad Pak

The *Mobile Launch Pad* was sold separately from the *Astro Trac Missile Convoy* set. The *Launch Pad* was a white plastic platform, 10" in length and about 5" at its widest. It had molded treads similar to the *Cat / Lunar Trac*, and looks similar to the base of an army tank. The platform was designed to hold the *Satellite Launcher*, *Space Probe* or *Rocket Launcher* in various configurations. Four thin wheels located on two axles allowed it to be pulled by the *Space Crawler*, *Uni-Tred* or *Astro Trac*. These motorized vehicles could work their way through almost any alien dunes. The mobile launch pad struggled

to get through that shag gold carpeting, its spindly wheels becoming entwined. This was actually a nondescript item becoming interesting only when included as part of the defensive capabilities when the *Launchers* were attached.

Gamma Ray Gard Pak

What a great toy! "Space probes combat radioactive materials and harmful gamma rays". This was a three-legged tripod base molded in bright red plastic jointed to pivot in almost any direction. The top of the *Gard* was a missile-type barrel molded in white plastic. The *Gamma Ray Gard* would fire mylar gold colored spikes at approaching space enemies. The missiles could be loaded into four barrels and, when turned, would fire out with great force. They were capable of traveling twenty five feet, yet wouldn't damage anything with a direct hit because of their flexible material. This was a unique toy since it fired the probes using their own compression from a tight fitting launch compartment. The *Gamma Ray Gard* is frequently found complete and in working condition since it had only three simple parts.

Part 2 - *Major Matt Mason*: Mattel's *Man In Space*

XRG - 1 Reentry Glider with Major Matt Mason

The *Glider* was advertised in the 1969 Mattel product catalogue. It allowed "*Major Matt Mason* to fly into space". The blister card encouraged junior astronauts to "pilot the *XRG-1 Glider*" stating that it would "streak through space, reenter the Earth's atmosphere, glide and land safely on Earth". In truth, the *Glider* couldn't reach into space, but, when *Major Matt Mason* or one of "the team" was placed in the see through cockpit, the *Glider* became weighted and, only then, would fly, rather well, through the house or backyard. This was a large vehicle with an equally large wing span and two 5" dorsal fins standing erect that helped to stabilize the ship while in flight.

The *XRG-1* Re-entry Glider

NASA concept glider which spawned the *XRG-1* design

Space Bubble

The *Space Bubble* was a great vehicle and I have vivid memories of this *Major Matt Mason* toy. The product catalogue stated that the *Space Bubble* enabled "astronauts to explore space and to travel into previously inaccessible regions". The *Space Bubble* could be "towed over lunar terrain, the Gyro-Seat Control Center remains upright as the *Space Bubble* rotates 360 degrees. The *Space Bubble* can be pulled or pushed by the *Uni-Tred*, *Astro Trac*, *Space Crawler* or *Firebolt Space Cannon*." The advertisements neglected to mention that the *Major* could also explore deep sea regions of extraterrestrial oceans much like a bathyscaphe. Many times the *Space Bubble* and its occupant went on deep sea exploration missions in the bathtub, coming up only when time ran out and the Great Sea Explorer had to go to his sleeping quarters for the night. The *Bubble* box art stated that "*Space Bubbles* could be hooked together to create convoy action."

Satellite Locker

Rear view of *Satellite Locker* with cardboard insert

The *Satellite Locker* was billed by Mattel as a "portable tote which stores up to three 6" astronauts and gear." It was made of "washable vinyl and featured a 'see-through' window, sturdy handle and lock".

The Battery Operated Mechanical Toys:

Talking Command Console

Heralded as Mattel's "first talking space toy", the 1969 merchandising catalogue proclaimed "Hear the astronaut conversations...Ready for Blast-off - 3...2...1! 10 exciting flight maneuvers in all, along with real space sounds!, Interior radar screens light with flashing colored signals while astronauts (not included) monitor from swivel-tilt console seats, 2-way vista window and simulated interior, Vinyl, battery operated." This toy was a "talkie" and spoke phrases when its cord was pulled. Most no longer work today since the rubber O rings have long since disintegrated.

Talking Command Console - Mattel's first talking space toy

Astro Trac

This was a "rugged mobile explorer with *Astro-foam* traction rear wheels. It was space designed for *Major Matt Mason, Sgt. Storm* and space scientists *Jeff Long* or *Doug Davis*." It resembled NASA's own lunar rover and was "battery-powered with front wheels that steer, space labels and instructions." This white plastic molded vehicle measured 7" in length. The *Astro Trac* can still be found today, and surprisingly many still operate although rarely do they have their foamed rear wheels which have usually long since disintegrated. Reproduction wheels are now being manufactured and can be purchased through a cottage industry that is springing up to supply common missing and damaged parts for the Mattel *Man in Space* line-up of toys. Mattel referred to their *Astro Trac* as the "mighty, mobile planet explorer, with universal *Astro-foam* traction wheels allowing it to skim dust dunes".

Space Crawler and early NASA concept moon crawler

Space Crawler

This was the *Major Matt Mason* vehicle of choice and my most used and abused *Major Matt Mason* toy. You couldn't stop this vehicle and it really could climb just

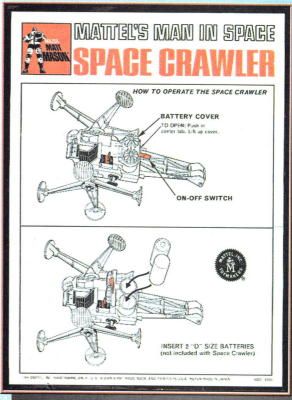

Part 2 - *Major Matt Mason*: Mattel's *Man In Space*

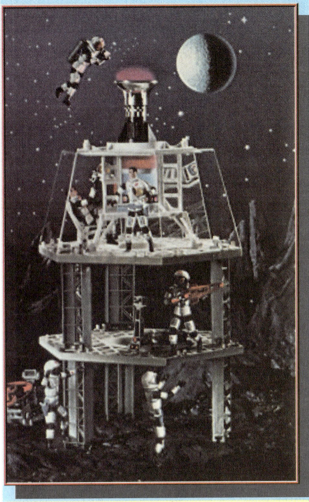

Mattel's *Space Station*

about anything. In fact, it was often tested to see just what it could do and with a little help, it *could* climb the stairs to the second floor. Alas, it came to an untimely end when the new puppy, still in its chewing anything in sight phase, chewed off a number of those spider-like leg / wheels, but it still ran! Mattel's description of this toy was right on as it stated "Invincible vehicle tracks over the roughest surface, defies gravity with rotating legs, raises and hauls supplies. Battery-powered with 2-way gears with winch action too"! After the *Crawler* could no longer roam the dark side of the moon, because of its unfortunate "accident", it sat atop the *Space Station*, using its functional engine and winch to raise and lower supplies and act as an elevator for astronauts wishing to access the command center.

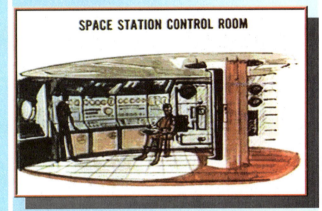

NASA concept space station control center

Space Station

The *Space Station* has been included here in the motorized toy section because the beacon sitting on top of the station was battery operated. Mattel stated that the *Space Station* was a "massive astral base with spectacular bi-level housing automatic flashing *Space Radar Beacon* and *Central Control Console*. Spacemen and space gear lock into platform grids." It came with other components including "space girders, space screws, 6 movable tinted solar shields, flight chair, vinyl ground sheet and space insignia." One of the great things about the *Space Station* was that it could be built in a number of configurations and, if you could convince your parents to buy you more that one, you could build a Super *Space Station*!. A number of accessories fit the *Space Station*. The aforementioned launchers could be

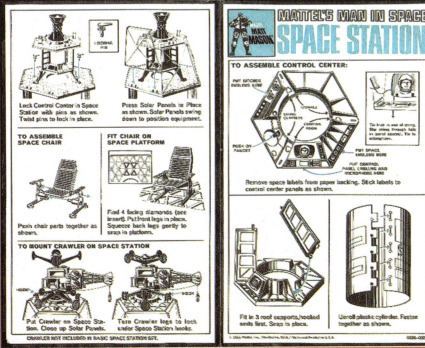

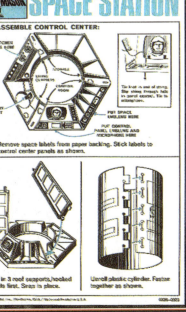

Part 2 - Major Matt Mason: Mattel's *Man In Space*

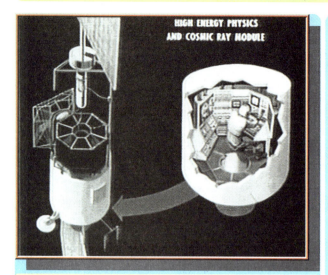

NASA concept orbital space station module

fitted to the *Station*, as could the *Space Crawler*. String operated vehicles like the *Reconojet* could be flown right into the *Space Station* for docking and, with the help of the string and red hooks of the *Jet Propulsion Pak* and *Talking Backpack*, the astronauts could move throughout the station and the lunar surface.

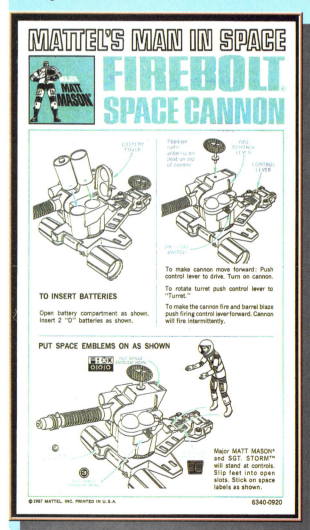

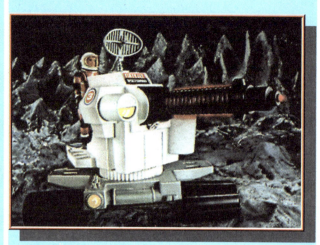

Firebolt Space Cannon

This was the only space vehicle that I didn't have as a child. It was very large and three wheeled and served to defend against alien attack. Mattel stated that the "whirling barrel transmits lazer energy and solar sound. The control screen blazes with light each time the lazer is released while the rotating turret and radar scanner seeks solar targets. It travels with *Captain Lazer* or *Major Matt Mason* and the other astronauts." The *Firebolt Space Cannon* came richly decaled and was molded with black wheels, red base and white turret with red radar dish.

Major Matt Mason wearing his *Talking Back Pack*

Part 2 - Major Matt Mason: Mattel's *Man In Space*

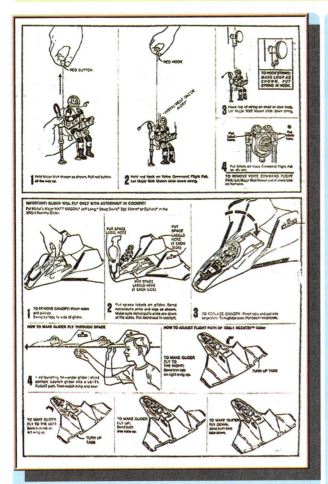

Instructions for using Matt with the *Talking Backpack* and *Glider*

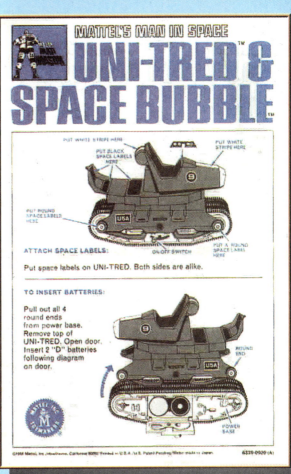

Talking Backpack

The brightly colored orange *Backpack* with silver / gray plastic landing legs could carry the famous *Major Matt Mason* from the *Lunar Command Base* or zoom across the surface of the moon. With the small red knobbed hook the *Major* could descend or fly and upon his return would state "Mission accomplished ! Returning to ship". He could say five phrases in total. Like the *Command Console*, the "O" rings in this item by now have disintegrated and most *Backpacks* no longer talk.

Uni-Tred Space Hauler

This was the fourth vehicle to be made for the *Major Matt Mason* space toy series. I begged my parents repeatedly for this and finally, on a return trip from Florida, they gave in. If the *Space Crawler* could go almost anywhere, then the *Uni-Tred* was likewise virtually unstoppable. It could go anywhere with its planetronic shift. The *Uni-Tred* was so technically advanced, to a nine-year-old, that it could even change gears when ascending cliffs. My favorite line from the advertising, and a stroke of shear brilliance, stated that the *Uni-Tred* could "bite into slippery surfaces with hundreds of space teeth!" The *Uni-Tred Space Hauler* operated on two D-size batteries. It operated by way of a large rubber tread that encircled the entire base of the toy. Sitting atop of the treaded base was a white plastic frame that was removable. It's primary purpose was to support the upper red plastic chassis where the *Major* and two of his buddies could sit.

Star Seeker

This was without a doubt the most unusual and mechanically complicated of the *Major Matt Mason* toys. It featured a "memory guidance system" which took me quite a while to figure out, since I didn't have this one when I was a kid! The ship was a capsule shape and only one of the astronaut figures could sit inside the blue canopy at a time. Below the figure compartment is a series of holes, a blue platform and orange hoses. When the hoses were put in the holes, the *Star Seeker* would

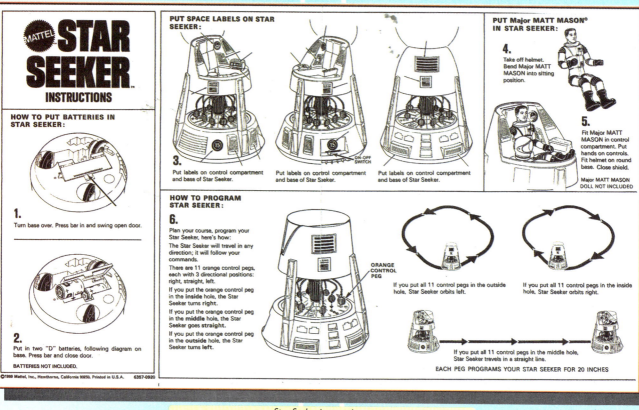

Star Seeker instructions

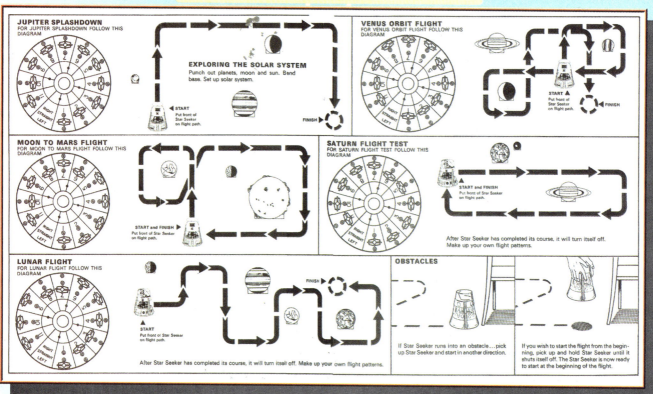

Star Seeker solar system planets

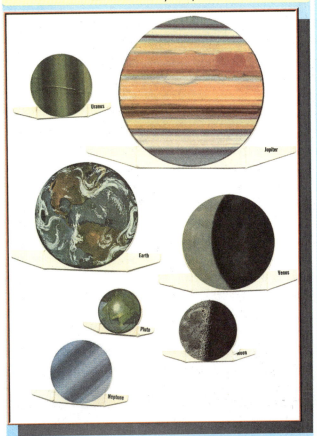

move about the floor in various driving patterns. Mattel provided the following descriptor in their advertisements "the *Star Seeker* glides forward on a path predicted by the 11 control pegs on the revolving Memory Guidance System. Each peg fits in one of the three positions, right, left or straight, in an endless number of combinations! Any Mattel astronaut rides safely in the Upper Control Deck, protected by a movable tinted shield, 11" tall, the *Star Seeker* turns off its battery power automatically, signaling the end of the mission." Create a circuit around our Solar System.

Orbitor

To my knowledge this item was not produced. It was displayed in Mattel product catalogues however. Mattel advertisements stated "Up . . up it soars, whirling toward a space adventure! Launch this unique spacecraft with a pull of the power cord — no batteries needed! OR! strange-shaped visitor from Orion pilots the 12-inch rotor from its central dome. Hi-impact plastic and steel launcher, Space decals included."

Catalogues, Wishbooks And Television Tie-Ins

Mattel Mini Catalogue

The 1966 Mattel *Major Matt Mason* mini catalogue that was included with some, but not all, of the *Major Matt Mason* boxed toys was actually a very colorful fold-out. It depicted the vast mountainous moonscape in the foreground. Photos of *Major Matt Mason* and his accessories appeared on the front cover in action mode. The *Space Sled* appeared to be gliding across the page with the *Space Crawler* roving the lunarscape. Opening the mini-catalogue revealed a brightly colored description of many of the space toys, which has been reproduced in this chapter, below. Described were a number of space accessories that helped the *Major* complete his outer space missions. Two small pictures were used on the inside of this catalogue, one of the *Space Crawler* and another of the *Space Station*. The same picture was used on the very large *Space Station* box. Flipping to the back of the catalogue were five more 2" thumb nail sized pictures of the *Rocket Launch Pak*, *Moon Suit Pak*, *Space Probe Pak*, *Space Ship Case* and *Major Matt Mason* wearing his *Jet Propulsion Pak*.

"MEET MAJOR MATT MASON, MATTEL'S MAN IN SPACE" invited Mattel toys. "All *Major Matt Mason's* equipment is based on official space program designs. This equipment must help him deal with violent temperature extremes, radiation, meteorites and strange rough terrain.

The moon is two hundred forty thousand miles away from earth and has no air, wind, or weather.

Mattel Mini Catalog cover

A day on earth is 24 hours — a "day" on the moon is one month. While the sun shines continuously for two weeks, temperatures soar to 250° F. During a "night" that lasts two weeks, temperatures drop to 250° below zero.

Because sprays of meteorites crash into the moon, *Major Matt Mason* will travel over knife-sharp rocks, over dust beds that may sink many feet deep, and will climb huge mountains. He will collect minerals and fossils.

The uniform of the day for *Major Matt Mason* is his *Space Suit*. It has a detachable helmet and movable, tinted visor. For his personal transportation, he has a *Space Sled*, which moves him across the moon's surface, or above it, with a short-range jet pack.

Major Matt Mason's Moon Suit gives him even more protection from the extreme temperature changes and radiation while exploring the planet and collecting samples. Other important equipment includes two *Launch Packs* with which *Major Matt Mason* can launch rockets and space probes into hard-to-reach areas.

For complete mobility on any planetary surface, *Major Matt Mason* has a strange looking but very practical *Space Crawler*. The *Crawler* is equipped with power-pads, which go over any kind of surface, even crevices. It lands back on its "feet" automatically if it is accidentally overturned. The *Space Crawler* can also be mounted on a hilltop or the *Space Station* and can be a powerful hoisting winch. The winch rotates in any direction after a load is lifted. The *Space Station* is *Major Matt Mason's* home in space. It provides living quarters as well as complete operations equipment for any length of time spend on a planet. The *Station* converts as a one or two story center or a separate moon base with two *space platforms*, six *space girders* and *control center*. The *control*

Part 2 - *Major Matt Mason*: Mattel's *Man In Space*

center is protected by swing-down tinted *Solar Panels*. A flashing *space beacon* signals to orbiting spacecraft, and tells earth that all is well. For interplanetary travel, *Major Matt Mason's Space Ship* is a sturdy, safe carrier for him and much of his equipment. Join us now for a great adventure into space with these exciting *Major Matt Mason* toys available wherever toys are sold.

SPACE CRAWLER

One of the most important vehicles for Major Matt Mason. Designed to do many jobs. It crawls over deep craters and crevices, sharp rocks, soft dust beds. Tows, pulls and hauls heavy equipment. Mounts on Space Station, works as an elevator for astronauts and supplies. When load reaches the pulley on the boom, the Space Crawler rotates, moving objects around the Space Station.   #6304

Also available: #6311 Space Crawler Action Set with Major Matt Mason.

SPACE STATION

Here, Major Matt and his crew keep radio contact with earth, plan moon explorations, direct space travels. Flashing beacon light guides space craft. Complete with radar, space platforms, space girders, control center, movable furniture, dome with swing-down Solar Panels. Can be set up many different ways.   #6308

Also available: #6310, Deluxe Action Set with Major Matt Mason, Space Station, Space Crawler.

ROCKET LAUNCH PAK

Launch pak mounts on Space Station or Moon Surface. Launches rockets that collect atmospheric samples and carry messages to earth. Includes walkie talkie, automatic rifle, knife and sheath.   #6305

Space Crawler

One of the most important vehicles for *Major Matt Mason*. Designed to do many jobs. It crawls over deep craters and crevices, sharp rocks, soft dust beds. Tows, pulls and hauls heavy equipment. Mounts on *Space Station*, works as an elevator for astronauts and supplies. When load reaches the pulley on the boom, the *Space Crawler* rotates, moving objects around the *Space Station*.

Space Station

Here, *Major Matt* and his crew keep radio contact with earth, plan moon explorations, direct space travels. Flashing beacon light guides spacecraft. Complete with *radar, space platforms, space girders, control center*, movable furniture, dome with swing-down *Solar Panels*. Can be set up many different ways.

Rocket Launch Pak

The *Rocket Launch Pak* mounts on the *Space Station* or the Lunar Surface. It launches rockets that collect atmospheric samples and carry messages to earth. Includes walkie-talkie, automatic rifle, knife and sheath.

SPACE PROBE PAK

Designed to probe the moon's surface and send information back to the main base. Adjusts for long or short distance firing. Complete with chemical gun, binoculars and flare signal.   #6307

Space Probe Pak

Designed to probe the moon's surface and send information back to the main base. Adjusts for long or short distance firing. Complete with chemical gun, binoculars and flare signal.

MAJOR MATT MASON
Major Matt Mason in space suit adapted from U.S. Apollo suit, to regulate oxygen supply and pressure. Includes space helmet with movable visor, Space Sled and remote control Jet Pak.   #6300

Major Matt Mason

Major Matt Mason in space suit adapted from the U.S. Apollo suit, to regulate oxygen supply and pressure, includes space helmet with movable visor, *Space Sled* and remote control *Jet Pak*.

MOON SUIT PAK

Adapted from U.S. Space program. You control flexible arm joints. Hammer, screw driver, wrench, radiation detector, too.   #6301

Also available: #6303 Major Matt Mason with MOON SUIT.

Moon Suit Pak

Adapted from U.S. Space program. You control flexible arm joints. Hammer, screwdriver, wrench, and radiation detector too.

SPACE SHIP CASE

Holds Major Matt Mason and space equipment. Has acceleration couch, pockets for small gear and equipment, carrying handle.   #6316

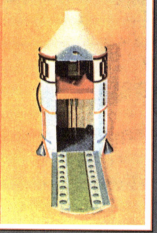

Space Ship Case

Holds *Major Matt Mason* and space equipment. Has acceleration couch, pockets for small gear and equipment, carry handle."

Company Product Catalogues

Mattel produced catalogues of their upcoming toy lines that were sent to potential buyers to allow them to view and order toys for their stores. The 1969 Mattel Toy Makers Spring Catalogue, on pages 51 through 56, contained many brightly colored pictures of the upcoming line of *Major Matt Mason* toys. This section of the catalogue was entitled Mattel's Man-in-Space Program (World of *Major Matt Mason*.) The first page is a full color picture of items available including; the *Flight Set, Reconojet Pak, Sgt. Storm, Space Station, Jeff Long, Doug Davis, Captain Lazer, Space Shelter, Gamma Ray Gard, Supernaut Power-Limbs* and *Space Power Suit Pak*. The following five pages contained detailed pictures and descriptions of the items listed above. Of note is that some of the toys differ from the actual production toy. The blue vista dome found on the *Space Power Suit* is not shown in blue, but rather clear plastic. All bendie astronauts are far more detailed than their production version. Each astronaut includes silver detailing on his boots with a stripe up the middle, silver around both leg cuffs and sleeve cuffs. Silver detailing

Part 2 - *Major Matt Mason*: Mattel's Man In Space

is shown on the figures at the neckline of each space suit, which is circled in black and then another small silver ring. The picture of *Callisto* shows him standing on a grainy blue moon surface. What is immediately noticeable is that he is a rough prototype and has the appearance of having been hand molded. The boots are rather crude looking and the hands lack detailing, such as fingers.

Mattel 1969 Spring Catalog pages 51- 52 (top) and 53 - 54 (bottom)

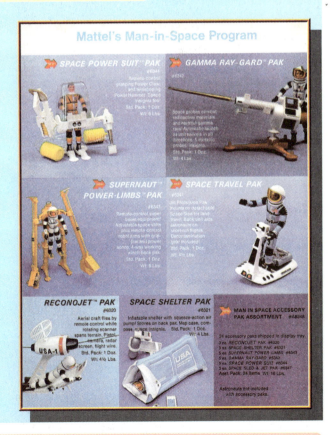

Mattel 1969 Spring Catalog pages 55 - 56

Mattel Doll and Toy Reference Guide 1970

The 1970 Mattel Toy Makers Quick Reference Guide contained descriptions and pictures of many of Mattel's toy lines including "Toys for Girls" — The World of Barbie, The World of Liddle Kiddles, Wet Noodles. It also listed "Toys for Boys and

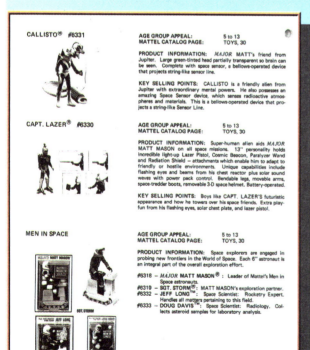

CALLISTO® #6331

AGE GROUP APPEAL: 5 to 13
MATTEL CATALOG PAGE: TOYS, 30

PRODUCT INFORMATION: *MAJOR MATT's* friend from Jupiter. Large green-tinted head partially transparent so brain can be seen. Complete with space sensor, a bellows-operated device that projects string-like sensor line.

KEY SELLING POINTS: CALLISTO is a friendly alien from Jupiter with extraordinary mental powers. He also possesses an amazing Space Sensor device, which senses radioactive atmospheres and materials. This is a bellows-operated device that projects a string-like Sensor Line.

CAPT. LAZER® #6330

AGE GROUP APPEAL: 5 to 13
MATTEL CATALOG PAGE: TOYS, 30

PRODUCT INFORMATION: Super-human alien aids *MAJOR MATT MASON* on all space missions. 13" personality holds incredible light-up Lazer Pistol, Cosmic Beacon, Paralyzer Wand and Radiation Shield — attachments which enable him to adapt to friendly or hostile environments. Unique capabilities include flashing eyes and beams from his chest reactor plus solar sound weves with power pack control. Bendable legs, movable arms, space-tredder boots, removable 3-D space helmet. Battery-operated.

KEY SELLING POINTS: Boys like CAPT. LAZER's futuristic appearance and how he towers over his space friends. Extra play-fun from his flashing eyes, solar chest plate, and lazer pistol.

MEN IN SPACE

AGE GROUP APPEAL: 5 to 13
MATTEL CATALOG PAGE: TOYS, 30

PRODUCT INFORMATION: Space explorers are engaged in probing new frontiers in the World of Space. Each 6" astronaut is an integral part of the overall exploration effort.

#6318 — *MAJOR MATT MASON®* : Leader of Mattel's Men in Space astronauts.
#6319 — SGT. STORM® : MATT MASON's exploration partner.
#6332 — JEFF LONG™ : Space Scientist: Rocketry Expert. Handles all matters pertaining to this field.
#6333 — DOUG DAVIS™ : Space Scientist: Radiology. Collects asteroid samples for laboratory analysis.

TALKING, FLYING
MAJOR **MATT MASON®** #6378

AGE GROUP APPEAL: 5 to 11
MATTEL CATALOG PAGE: TOYS, 32

PRODUCT INFORMATION: *MAJOR* MATT MASON flies into space and tells junior astronauts his reactions with his VOICE COMMAND FLIGHT PAK. No batteries needed to operate the removable VOICE COMMAND FLIGHT PAK. *MAJOR* MATT MASON has he flies, with realistic space sound effects.

KEY SELLING POINTS: A popular toy for boys, *MAJOR* MATT MASON now talks and flies in his space travels to add new dimension to play value. The VOICE COMMAND FLIGHT PAK may be used with any of Mattel's astronauts who assist *MAJOR* MATT MASON in the exciting exploration of space.

STAR SEEKER™ #6357

AGE GROUP APPEAL: 5 to 11
MATTEL CATALOG PAGE: TOYS, 28

PRODUCT INFORMATION: STAR SEEKER with memory guidance system will transport *MAJOR* MATT MASON and his Men in Space to more than 100,000 different inter-stellar routes. Battery-operated, the STAR SEEKER looks like an Apollo ship: the white sturdy plastic vehicle carries any Mattel astronaut in the Upper Control Deck with a tinted, movable shield. The blue program wheel with orange memory pegs rotates while STAR SEEKER is on a mission.

KEY SELLING POINTS: STAR SEEKER remembers commands. Each memory peg fits in a right, left or straight position and the 11 pegs can program an endless number of combinations for extra-terrestrial exploration. The sun, moon and 9 stand-up planets are included with STAR SEEKER so boys can plot and navigate their own star voyages. STAR SEEKER can be programmed to return to its starting point or to roam at random. Battery power is turned off automatically to signal the end of mission.

SCORPIO™ #6359

AGE GROUP APPEAL: 5 to 11
MATTEL CATALOG PAGE: TOYS, 29

PRODUCT INFORMATION: SCORPIO, an unusual alien creature with flashing eyes and mouth, joins CALLISTO and CAPT. LAZER, outer-space friends of *MAJOR* MATT MASON and his space crew.

KEY SELLING POINTS: SCORPIO resembles a humanoid insect, wearing removable arm and leg armor. Battery inside his body cavity powers his blinking eyes and mouth. He wears a back-pack vest projector which propels search globes into space. Vest projector is operated by a bellows system. SCORPIO is bendable and posable. Search globes are safe styrofoam.

BOYS

Part 2 - *Major Matt Mason:* **Mattel's *Man In Space***

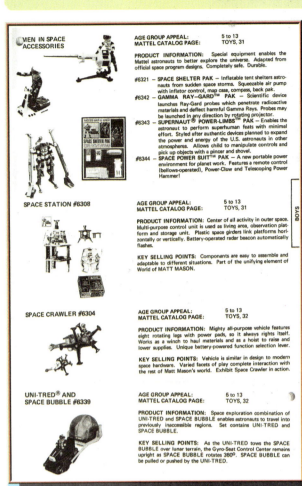

MEN IN SPACE ACCESSORIES

AGE GROUP APPEAL: 5 to 13
MATTEL CATALOG PAGE: TOYS, 31

PRODUCT INFORMATION: Special equipment enables the Mattel astronauts to better explore the universe. Adapted from official space program designs. Completely safe. Durable.

#6321 – SPACE SHELTER PAK – Inflatable tent shelters astronauts from sudden space storms. Squeezable air pump with inflator control, map case, compass, back pak.

#6342 – GAMMA RAY-GARD™ PAK – Scientific device launches Ray-Gard probes which penetrate radioactive materials and deflect harmful Gamma Rays. Probes may be launched in any direction by rotating projector.

#6343 – SUPERNAUT® POWER-LIMBS™ PAK – Enables the astronaut to perform superhuman feats with minimal effort. Styled after authentic devices planned to expand the power and energy of the U.S. astronauts in other atmospheres. Allows child to manipulate controls and pick up objects with a pincer and shovel.

#6344 – SPACE POWER SUIT™ PAK – A new portable power environment for planet work. Features a remote control (bellows-operated), Power-Claw and Telescoping Power Hammer!

SPACE STATION #6308

AGE GROUP APPEAL: 5 to 13
MATTEL CATALOG PAGE: TOYS, 31

PRODUCT INFORMATION: Center of all activity in outer space. Multi-purpose control unit is used as living area, observation platform and storage unit. Plastic space girders link platforms horizontally or vertically. Battery-operated radar beacon automatically flashes.

KEY SELLING POINTS: Components are easy to assemble and adaptable to different situations. Part of the unifying element of World of MATT MASON.

SPACE CRAWLER #6304

AGE GROUP APPEAL: 5 to 13
MATTEL CATALOG PAGE: TOYS, 32

PRODUCT INFORMATION: Mighty all-purpose vehicle features eight rotating legs with power pads, so it always rights itself. Works as a winch to haul materials and as a hoist to raise and lower supplies. Unique battery-powered function selection lever.

KEY SELLING POINTS: Vehicle is similar in design to modern space hardware. Varied facets of play complete interaction with the rest of Matt Mason's world. Exhibit Space Crawler in action.

UNI-TRED® AND SPACE BUBBLE #6339

AGE GROUP APPEAL: 5 to 13
MATTEL CATALOG PAGE: TOYS, 32

PRODUCT INFORMATION: Space exploration combination of UNI-TRED and SPACE BUBBLE enables astronauts to travel into previously inaccessible regions. Set contains UNI-TRED and SPACE BUBBLE.

KEY SELLING POINTS: As the UNI-TRED tows the SPACE BUBBLE over lunar terrain, the Gyro-Seat Control Center remains upright as SPACE BUBBLE rotates 360°. SPACE BUBBLE can be pulled or pushed by the UNI-TRED.

BOYS

Mattel 1970 Toy Reference Guide (above and previous page)

Girls", with such items as Upsy Downsy, Skeddiddler, Talking Cuddle Snuggles, Mattel-O-Phones, Thingmakers and Wiz-z-zer Whirlers. In the section "Toys for Boys", the Toy Reference Guide listed such memorable favorites as Sea Devils, Hot Wheels, Ramrod Western Guns and Long Ranger Guns. In this section, under the heading World of Space, was the *Major Matt Mason* toy lineup, filled with small black and white photos of additions to the *Major Matt Mason* line. Within four pages, of this 40 page catalogue, could be found the latest additions including the *Talking Flying Major Matt Mason*, *Star Seeker*, *Scorpio*, *Callisto* (still using the prototype photograph), *Captain Lazer*, *Sgt. Storm*, *Jeff Long*, *Doug Davis*, *Space Shelter*, *Gamma Ray*, *Supernaut Power-Limbs* and *Space Power Paks*. Also included in the small 2" photographs were the *Space Station*, *Space Crawler* and finally the *Uni-Tred and Space Bubble*. Interesting to note, there is no mention of *Or* and his *Orbitor* in the 1970 Quick Toy Reference Guide.

Store Wishbooks

Department store catalogues and Christmas Wishbooks are a wonderful place to locate information, original prices and details of accessories for your favorite childhood toy, and *Major Matt Mason* toys are no exception. Simpson-Sears stores, Gambles, J.C Penny, Montgomery Ward, Toy City, K Mart, Zellers, Eatons, Woolco, The Right House, Robinson's and Canadian Tire are just a few places to start looking. Most department stores put together large toy sections in their Christmas Wishbooks, and if you review these 1967 through 1970 catalogues you'll be sure to find *Major Matt Mason* items. The Sears Wishbook for 1968 ran black and white pages showing the rare *Launch Pad* vehicle. The 1969 Wishbook ran color full-page ads of the *Uni-Tred Space Hauler* and *Astro Trac*. J.C. Penny featured all the *Major Matt Mason* inventory with pictures and prices of, among other items, the *Space Mission Team*. Here an eager little astronaut could receive, if he could talk his mother into it, the four man set (*Mason*, *Davis*, *Storm* and *Long*) with *Space Sled* and *Cat Trac* for a mere $6.44. Today, that set will cost you a handsome $600.00, a one-thousand percent increase! In these days of buy-outs, mergers and mutual funds, don't we wish we all had a few cases of these items set aside in the attic. The Montgomery

Gambles Matt Mason toys

Part 2 - *Major Matt Mason*: Mattel's *Man In Space*

Ward 1970 catalogue introduced the *Uni-Tred Space Hauler, Space Bubble* and *Major Matt Mason's* "amazing *Star Seeker.*" Notice that in the Canadian *Major Matt Mason* advertisement for the *XRG-1 Glider* and *Callisto* figure sold for $3.49. The ad shows a young boy throwing the *Glider* through the air with *Callisto* at the

helm. The ad for this rare and unusual item reads '*Matt Mason XRG-1 Glider.* Launch it and watch it come back into the atmosphere. Well balanced for high flying and soft landing. Comes complete with *Matt Mason* outer space friend, *Callisto*, the alien with the bellow action sensor. 27-R 3078 - 18" long, 16" wide.'

Canadian advertisement for the *XRG-1 Glider* including *Callisto*

(right) Toy City newspaper advertisement - Note the prices!

Target Selling and Television Tie-ins

Mattel utilized print ads as well as thirty second television commercial spots to sell their line of Matt Mason toy figures and accessories. They also frequently used D.C Comics as a vehicle to sell toys. Many ads were run monthly in 1967 when *Matt Mason* and his space team were launched. Often times, as in the September 1967 issue, Mattel Toys included a full toy page illustrated ad. Mattel often included a one-page comic of the adventures of *Major Matt Mason*. On the adjacent page would follow a review of the product line with descriptions of the action figures, vehicles and action play sets. The review of each of the featured toys was taken, most often, from the Mattel Mini Catalogue descriptions. Throughout Mattel's production of *Major Matt Mason: Man in Space*, the company ran regular print advertisements in LIFE MAGAZINE. This coincided nicely with the many real NASA ads, articles, editorials and photographs. As an interesting aside, their suave ability to utilize various mediums of advertising certainly underscores Mattel's keen marketing skills — their comic book ads were always artist renditions of toys, like the

Mattel *Man In Space* advertisement run in Life Magazine

Part 2 - *Major Matt Mason*: Mattel's *Man In Space*

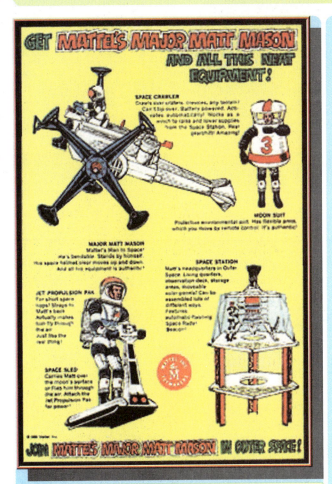

Mattel *Man In Space* illustrated advertisement in a comic book

Corey, Earl and their *Space Station* on the *Julia* TV series

comic book illustrations, whereas, in contrast, when appealing to adult buyers (parents and older youths) Mattel most often used full color photography enhancing the "authentic" look of the NASA design-based toys. Mattel, quick to jump into the television advertising medium with *Major Matt Mason* toys, ran numerous thirty second advertising spots. As with much advertising at the time, the *Major Matt Mason* toys and figures, such as the *Space Crawler* and *Talking Back Pak*, seemed to come to life on the lunar surface. Another television tie-in, *Major Matt* began showing up in the late 1960's and early 1970's television shows. Often times, if you looked carefully, you could see *Man in Space* toys occupying the bedroom shelves of Corey's bedroom in the television series, *Julia* starring Diahann Caroll. In the television series *Dark Shadows*, a young boy actor also has a *Major Matt Mason Space Station* and *Crawler* on a shelf in his bedroom, as does Eddie, as memory serves me, from the television series starring the late Bill Bixby, *The Courtship of*

Eddie's Father. A present day television tie-in is *The Rosie O'Donnell Show*, starring Ms. O'Donnell, which features various celebrities and personalities in a talk show format. Recently Rosie O'Donnell's featured guest Tom Hanks who, in his conversation with Rosie, mentioned the fact that *Major Matt Mason* was his favorite childhood toy, while another celebrity actor, Matthew Brodrick, was presented with a *Major Matt Mason* toy figure on *Rosie O'Donnell's* after he identified that this too was his favorite toy while growing up. Lastly on one other episode of the *Rosie O'Donnell Show*, Ms. O'Donnell queried both the television and studio audiences asking anyone if they remembered the *Zeroid Robot* series of toys from the late 1960's, when she professed having had an interest in them as a child (and, of course, I e-mailed her information and pictures through her on-line web page.) Rosie O'Donnell has most certainly raised the profile of television nostalgia collectable toys through her on-going discussions and displays of her personal collection and childhood anecdotes, and I thank her for furthering the interest in these long forgotten childhood toys.

Another Mattel *Man In Space* advertisement run in *Life Magazine*

Part 2 - *Major Matt Mason*: Mattel's *Man In Space*

Variations On A Theme

During the run of any toy line, variations of toys will occur, whether due to scaling down costs (e.g. less paint detailing equals less cost equals increased profit) or from various grades and colors of manufacturing materials being used. These variations can affect the desirability of collectable toys, and may, in fact, cause a particular toy to become collectable. In some cases, the "variation" can become highly sought after and prized among collectors. Toys may be re-engineered if a fault is found with an initial design. Often times, a toy will be modified to attract new buyers, as a low cost alternative to designing a new toy. Within the *Major Matt Mason* line of toys, numerous variations can be found. In this chapter you will find variations of all known toys, action figures and vehicles.

Foreign toys and boxes / bubble blister cards are covered later in their own chapter.

If you're looking for variations of *Major Matt Mason* toys, beware — the Mattel Toy Company didn't always have its "products" ready to show their merchandisers. As a result, in some of their dealer catalogues and mini catalogues, you may find color and mold variations on some items. For the most part, these items **were not** produced as shown. The *Space Station* is a case in point — the photographs that were shown to dealers differ from the actual toy produced. Sometimes, Mattel used pictures of both a prototype toy (a gray plastic / clear vista domed station) and the actual red and white molded station on the same box artwork. These variations, both produced and photographed, are discussed in the following chapter.

Talking Command Console - 1969

Command Console Variation
There are two known versions of this toy. The *Talking Command Console* was made with the "vista" window to the right of the moon showing a clear, non-colored see-through window.

Command Console Variation
Another variation of the *Command Console* was made with a dark blue see-through "vista window".

Command Console Decal Variation
Decal detailing was altered during production. *Talking Command Consoles* were predominately made with blue with black stripped decaled chairs and blue instead of black console stickers. Others decal details have been reported as being primarily black decaled chairs and blue console stickers.

Major Matt Mason - 1967

Major Matt Mason Variation
The initial production version of *Major Matt Mason* was a white rubberized plastic. Onto the white rubber was painted space suit details such as black "accordion" joints, silver painted sleeve cuffs and leg cuffs, blue harness straps, and large red dots located just above both wrists and at both leg shins.

Major Matt Mason Variation
Matt Mason was changed to black rubber molding painted with a glossy white. The "accordion" joints

were now unpainted. There were numerous detailing changes to the figures, including a blue harnessed *Matt Mason* with the red dots on both wrists and shin areas with black, unpainted cuffs and shin areas.

Major Matt Mason Variation
One other variation of *Matt Mason* included a blue harnessed figure without red dots and unpainted cuffs.

Major Matt Mason Variation
Major Matt Mason was detailed with blue straps, red dots on the shins and cuffs, and silver painting on the shins and cuffs as well.

The two head variations of *Major Matt Mason*

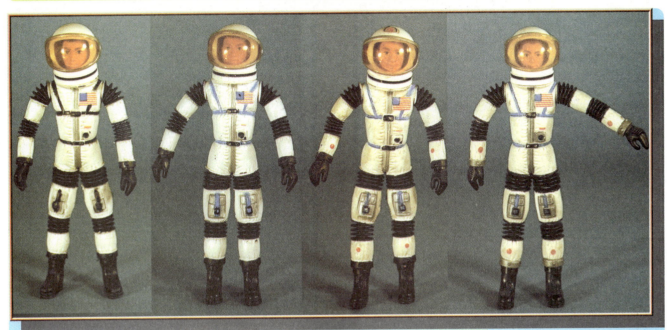

Various detailing variations on *Major Matt Mason*

Major Matt Mason Variation

The last variation I am aware of at the time of writing this reference guide is a black harnessed *Matt Mason* with unpainted black wrist and leg cuffs and no red dots.

Major Matt Mason Head Variation

Variations also occurred throughout the production run with regard to *Major Matt Mason* heads. I have in my collection two different sized *Matt Mason* heads. As well, Mattel molded the larger of the two heads with a darker complexion, it would appear, later in production.

Major Matt Mason Helmet Variation

Helmets varied for the Mattel astronaut toy line. There are two types of helmet decals. Some helmets, most likely the earlier version, have the black stripe at the opening of the helmet painted on, while later helmets make do with a thin black decal. Finally, there are two different number 3's that were used on the *Matt Mason* helmets. Some have the number three directly above the visor, while others do not. I, again, have seen number 3 printed in white with a black dot surrounding the designation. I have a larger three designation printed in red writing, surrounded by white and with a black border around the circumference of the round helmet decal. Number 2's were also applied directly to early *Matt* helmets at the factory.

A special note on the following figures of *Sgt. Storm*, *Doug Davis* and *Jeff Long* — In reviewing the various dealer catalogues that I've been fortunate enough to locate, it can clearly be seen that the initial photographs of these figures were repainted *Major Matt Mason*

figures. In some of the pictures, the heads can clearly be viewed. These figures were shown to be far more detailed than those produced, including silver painted zippers, silver highlighted boots, silver cuffs, and silver with black rings at the neckline.

Sgt. Storm - 1968

Detailing variations on *Sgt. Storm*

Part 2 - *Major Matt Mason*: Mattel's Man In Space

Sgt. Storm Variation

Sgt. Storm was introduced in year two of the Mattel's *Man in Space* toy production. There are a number of variations of this red space suited "bendie" figure. *Sgt. Storm*, *Matt Mason*'s space buddy, was manufactured with paint detailing that included black straps, white zipper, and black cuffs and shins without red dots.

Sgt. Storm Variation

Matt Mason's space buddy also, as a first issue, came with blue straps, white painted cuffs, white zipper, white shins, and black dots on the wrists and shin areas.

Sgt. Storm Variation

The *Sgt.* was painted with blue straps, no painting on the cuffs or shins with black dots on wrists only.

Sgt. Storm Variation

I have in my collection a *Sgt. Storm* that is detailed with black straps, no wrist or shin painting, and a silver colored zipper.

One further variation of the *Sgt. Storm* figure is on the connecting port to the right of his front suit zipper. In my collection I have the square areas detailed in red, silver and white.

Sgt. Storm Head Variations

As with the *Major Matt Mason* figure, *Sgt. Storm* has a large headed and smaller headed version. He was also manufactured with two complexion colors, a very light skinned face and a slightly tanned skin complexion.

Sgt. Storm Helmet Ring Variation

I've discovered that there are at least two variations of paint detailing at the helmet ring area. Some *Sgt. Storms* were manufactured with only red paint on this snap area, while others will have a silver painted ring area with white paint detailing under where the helmet fits.

Doug Davis - 1969

Doug Davis Variation

Doug Davis was manufactured wearing a yellow suit on some "bendie" figures, while on others his suit has an orange / yellow hue. Figures that I've found to date include black strapping, white zippers, and white knee patches detailed in black and silver. *Doug Davis* figures may have white paint detailing to add to the contours of his lips, but may not be highlighted in this area as well. I have both versions.

Jeff Long - 1969

Jeff Long Variation

Jeff Long - "Space Scientist - Rocketry expert" was the final astronaut to be manufactured for Mattel's *Man in Space* toy line. I am aware of no variations of this figure other than, similar to *Doug Davis*, minor hue differences in suit paint color. *Jeff Long*'s blue space suit can be found ranging from a light blue to darker, almost navy, blue. *Jeff*'s suit includes black straps, white zipper, and white patches with black and silver details.

Callisto - 1969

Callisto was made with short and long boots

Callisto Variation

Callisto, "*Major Matt Mason*'s friend from Jupiter" has a short list of variations. *Callisto* was manufactured with both short and tall boots, which permit him to tower over the shorter astronauts. *Callisto* with the tall boots is often referred to as the "platform *Callisto*." This figure is shown in the Mattel Toys Spring 1969 Catalogue clearly as a prototype. He is roughly molded with a yellow wire rather than yellow knotted string for the described "coil-action *Space Sensor*.

Callisto Variation

There are variations in the molds that were used by Mattel for the *Callisto* figures. One notable difference is that the blue colored bracelet that circles round his wrists on some *Callisto* figures touch, while on others the circles are much smaller and don't touch each other.

Callisto Variation

Paint variations occur on the *Callisto* figures also. The blue detailing on the top of the boots may be painted in either a V shape or in a straight line just touching the top of the boot. Hue variations, especially of the blue body accents, occurred from time to time. There are at least three versions of eyebrows, which range from very bushy and long to a shorter, more restrained design. Eye paint can change from *Callisto* to *Callisto*. Some have their eyes outlined in black, while others have black outlining only on the top of the lid.

Callisto head variation with bushy brows and black eye outlining

Callisto Variation

I am aware of two styles of *Callisto* heads, and possibly a third. The first *Callisto* head is molded from a see through green rubber. It's transparent enough that the snap which the head fits onto can be seen. The second style of *Callisto* head is molded from a more opaque, less jelly-like green rubber. I have pictures of a third molded *Callisto* head in a red opaque color, which I have included here, however, whether this is a true variation or a chemical reaction within the plastic of the head remains unknown at this time.

Scorpio - 1970

Scorpio

Scorpio was designed near the end of *Man in Space* manufacturing and only came in one style, with no variations of the North American item. *Scorpio* sported a hot pink body with inner torso, legs and arms and removable head. His hard body shell was molded in purple as were his shin and arm guards.

Captain Lazer - 1968

Captain Lazer

Captain Laser was fitted with anti-gravity *tredders*, molded in gray plastic, which clipped onto the bottoms of his boots. He came with a fitted gray plastic removable helmet. Although in one dealer catalogue he appears to be wearing a white angular helmet, on closer examination, this helmet has been painted into the

photograph. This helmet, I would conclude, is not a variation and doesn't exist. Fitting into *Captain Lazer*'s molded, silver painted gun were three wand attachments. There were numerous color combinations for the *radiation shield*, *paralyzer wand* and *cosmic beacon*, with any one of them being any of amber, purple or aqua in color. *Captain Lazer*'s backpack was molded in silver / gray plastic. His belt, molded gloved hands, and gun were detailed in the silver colored paint. The *Captain*'s eyes also were molded in colors amber, purple and aqua.

Copyright Lettering

Just as the *Major Matt Mason* line of astronauts went through numerous paint variations, they had variations also of the copyright detail. Both variations were large lettering stating "1966 Mattel Inc. US and Foreign patents pending."

Astronaut Helmets - 1967

The rare short neck and common long neck helmets

Helmet Variation

The initial helmet variation, molded in white plastic with a clear amber colored visor and silver outline, included a black painted ring on the base of the helmet. If you look closely, you'll see that the helmet has a short "neck" preceding the black stripping of the helmet opening.

Helmet Variation

The later helmet variation continues with the same white plastic molding with amber visor and silver detailing, but this helmet makes use of a black decal to stripe the helmet. The "neck" of the helmet is taller than the earlier produced helmet. I currently have 40 *Major Matt Mason* figures in my collection, with only three wearing the earlier, shorter helmets. I would conclude that the short-necked helmet is the much rarer of the two helmet variations.

Space Sled - 1967

Space Sled Variation
The initial *Space Sled* was a frequently used accessory for many of the *Major Matt Mason* toys. It was included in both carded packs and boxed sets. The first *Space Sled* consisted of two molded plastic pieces, a white case and column section that allowed the *Major* to hold onto grips. The grips in the initial toy design were small and thin handled, and appear very fragile.

Space Sled Variation
Sometime early in production, the grips of the *Space Sled* were altered. The later (and much more common) grips are made of thicker plastic, which is ribbed. They appear to be more substantial and I suspect less prone to breakage than the initially designed grips.

Moon Suit Pak - 1967

Moon Suit Pak
The *Moon Suit Pak* was a NASA designed suit that was meant to help *Major Matt Mason* explore the outer reaches of the galaxy. It included bellow operated flexible arms. There are no known variations of this item. The Mattel retail catalogues do show accessories (rock hammer, screwdriver and wrench) different from the actual production silver chromed versions. These "prototype" tools are of a different design.

Astro Trac - 1967

Astro Trac
The *Astro Trac* is not known to have had any variations throughout its product run. It continued on as a white plastic, molded vehicle with "*Astro-foam* traction wheels".

Major Matt Mason With Moon Suit - 1967

Moon Suit
As far as I'm aware, there are no *Moon Suit* variations. The *Moon Suit* did come with various *Major Matt Mason* figure variations.

Space Crawler - 1967

Space Crawler
The motorized *Space Crawler* with "powerful hoister and winch" design was altered from the original design. The initial design did not include a small oil hole to self-lubricate the motor. Further variations involved the red roller that fits on the underside of the tail section of the *Crawler*. Both variations were molded of red plastic. There is a smooth surface version and a rough surfaced

variation.

Satellite Launch Pak - 1967

Satellite Launch Pak
The *Satellite Launcher* fired, "with tremendous thrust", colorful *satellites*, high into the sky. There are no known variations of this item.

Space Station - 1967

Space Station
The *Space Station* was an elaborate and intricately detailed station that housed the *Major*, and his astronaut space buddies and alien friends. The only variation of the station is the inclusion of three support holes in the roof structure. These support holes, into which the *Command Console* fits, attached the roof structure more securely to the *Command Center*. In my collection, I have two color variations for the command chair.

Chair Variation
One chair is molded in white plastic with blue paint detailing in the cushion area.

Chair Variation
The second chair is strictly molded in the same white plastic, but is not detailed with the blue highlights as in the first chair variation.

Special Note:
The illustration of the *Space Station* that's included on the exterior of the box shows silver / gray strut supports and "clear" windows. This was a prototype and was not produced. I would suggest that perhaps the original coloring for the toy was thought to be

unattractive to the buying public, and the colors were changed to appeal to consumers. It has also been suggested that originally Mattel may have been attempting to remain true to the NASA space program and choose appropriate "real" colors for the station.

Space Crawler Action Set - 1967

Space Crawler Action Set
This action set included a *Major Matt Mason* figure, *Space Sled, Jet Propulsion Pak* and *Space Crawler*. Variations may have carried over from the individual items as sold separately.

Space Ship Carrying Case - 1967

Space Ship Carrying Case
There are no known variations with the *Space Ship Carrying Case*. The prototype of this item depicted the astronaut launch couch colored in an orange / red color. The production version of the launch couch was colored in dark blue vacuum-formed plastic.

Sgt. Storm Flight Pak - 1968

Sgt. Storm Flight Pak
As indicated, *Sgt. Storm* was produced in numerous variation configurations, which will be included on this *Flight Pak* card.

Major Matt Mason With Cat Trac - 1968

Matt Mason / Cat Trac
As indicated, *Major Matt Mason* was produced with numerous variations which may be included on his *Flight Pak* card.

Sgt. Storm With Cat Trac - 1968

Storm / Cat Trac
Sgt. *Storm* figures varied in production as indicated.

Reconojet Pak - 1968

Reconojet
There are no known variations of the *Reconojet Pak*.

Space Shelter Pak - 1968

Space Shelter
There are no known variations of the *Space Shelter* or accessories *Pak*.

Satellite Locker - 1968

Satellite Locker
The *Satellite Locker* came with a "life-size" 6" *Major Matt Mason* figure card insert that slipped into the window section of the locker.

Astro Trac Missile Convoy Set - 1968

Missile Convoy Set
This item was sold as a SEARS store exclusive. It is extremely rare and highly sought. There are no known variations of this item.

Mobile Launch Pad Pak - 1968

Mobile Launch Pad
This *Launch Pad* was used with the SEARS set. There are no known variations of the *Launch Pad*. This is a rare item and highly sought.

Uni-Tred And Space Bubble - 1969

Uni-Tred / Space Bubble Pak
This two piece set includes the same variations as for the two main toys as sold separately — i.e. different bubble tints, etc. I have, in my personal collection, a blue tinted bubble, gray tinted bubble, and clear tinted bubble with purple hue. Sometimes, the two halves of the bubble are different colors, as is the door section.

Major Matt Mason And Space Power Suit - 1969

Matt Mason / Space Power Suit
The "bendie" figure included with the *Space Power Suit* could be any of the variations listed above.

Firebolt Space Cannon - 1968

Firebolt Space Cannon
There are no known variations of the *Firebolt Space Cannon*. The illustration on the *Firebolt* box shows a *Cannon* with a silver base. This variation was a prototype and wasn't mass-produced.

Firebolt Space Cannon Super Action Set - 1968

Firebolt Space Cannon Super Action Set
This set included *Captain Lazer*, which, when sold separately, could be purchased with any number of variations as listed.

Part 2 - *Major Matt Mason*: Mattel's Man In Space

Gamma Ray Gard Pak - 1969

Gamma Ray Gard Pak
There are no known variations of the *Gamma Ray Gard*.

Supernaut Power Limb Pak - 1969

Power Limbs
There are no known variations of the *Power Limbs* toy accessory.

Space Power Suit - 1969

Space Power Suit
There are no known variations of this *Major Matt Mason* accessory toy. However, the dealer catalog does show a different shovel variation which has multiple ribbing at the end, whereas the final production version has only one middle rib. As well, the blue "vista dome" that was produced is shown in many dealer catalogues as a clear see-through dome

Space Bubble - 1969

Space Bubble
There are numerous color combinations of the *Space Bubble*. The clear plastic used to produce the bubble section has been reported in a clear / purple color, blue color, and gray color. It's not uncommon to encounter a bubble which consists of two half shells and the escape hatch which are molded in various combinations of color.

Unit-Tred Space Hauler - 1969

Uni-Tred
There are no known variations of this motorized lunar transport vehicle.

Space Travel Pak - 1969

Space Travel Pak
There are no known variations of this *Major Matt Mason* accessory.

Captain Lazer Firebolt Space Cannon Action Set - 1969

Captain Lazer / Firebolt Action Set
This Action Set includes the previously listed variations of *Captain Lazer*. Any one of the many color combinations of *Captain Lazer* could be found with this particular action set.

Lunar Base Command Set - 1969

Lunar Base Command Set
The *Lunar Base Command Set* includes only previously listed variations of *Callisto*, the *Space Bubble* and *Major Matt Mason*. It's possible that the initial variation of the *Space Station* may have found its way into the initial production boxes of this toy.

Space Discovery Set - 1969

Space Discovery Set
This *Space Discovery Set*, including the *Space Crawler*, *Callisto* and *Space Bubble*, could include any number of the known variations, as listed separately.

Star Seeker - 1970

Star Seeker
There are no known variations produced for this toy.

XRG-1 Reentry Glider - 1969

Reentry Glider
The *Reentry Glider* was produced with a number of variations. There are two canopies for the *Glider*, and three color variations of the same canopy. The initial design of the canopy was a totally removable plastic, see-through piece fitted with a "dimple" in the nose of the ship into which the front of the canopy fit. The rear of the canopy had two cutouts that fit into two slots in the white vacuum-formed *Glider*. The second canopy was fitted with a rivet instead of front "dimple" and was slightly smaller. The color of the canopy varied in the same manner as the color of the *Space Bubble*. There are known color variations of blue, gray / purple, and clear transparent canopies.

XRG-1 Reentry Glider With Major Matt Mason - 1969

Reentry Glider With Major Matt Mason
Known variations include only those previously listed for both *Major Matt Mason* and the *Glider*.

Talking Major Matt Mason - 1970

Talking Matt Mason
This item included both the *Major* and his talking orange *Back Pack*. There are no known variations of the *Talking Back Pack*.

Part 2 - *Major Matt Mason*: Mattel's Man In Space

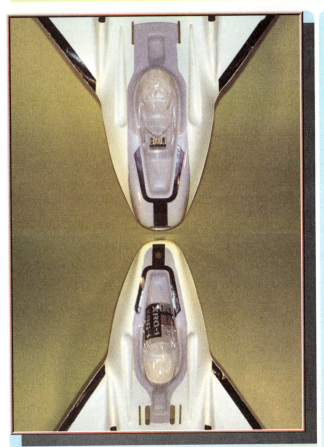

XRG-1 *Glider* with removable (top) and riveted canopies

Talking Major Matt Mason With
XRG-1 Reentry Glider - 1970

Matt Mason / Propulsion Pak / Glider
Known variations of this toy are those listed for the individual items as sold separately.

Major Matt Mason Space Power
Equipment Set - 1970

Power Equipment Set
There are no known variations of this toy.

Star Seeker Walk in Space Set - 1970

Star Seeker Walk in Space Set
There are no known variations of this boxed set.

Paper Products and Spin-Offs

The *Major Matt Mason: Man in Space* toy line spanned numerous non-toy spin-offs. Among the many items were paper products, puzzles, a board game, three ring school binder, children's wallet, coloring book, press out activity book, child's novel, lunch box, wallpaper and Halloween costume.

The Mattel Toy company manufactured a *Major Matt Mason* wallet made of vinyl. The wallet showed an artist's illustration of *Major Matt Mason* floating in deep space above his space capsule. This wallet is scarce, but has been produced, and was not just as a prototype, as some collector's believe. The *Major Matt Mason* Space Exploration game was made of plastic and was molded to represent the moon's surface. The game utilized those *Man in Space* graphics that we love so much of the *Major* in various action moves and driving or riding various space vehicles. The Mattel three ring binder is extremely scarce. This plastic binder was produced in 1969 and utilized the same graphic as the *Man in Space* Wallet. The Mattel Toy Company was not alone in producing spin-off paper products for *Major Matt*. Whitman books, a.k.a. Western Publishing, produced a number of colorful and exciting *Major Matt Mason* paper items. Their Big Little book series, which included dozens of titles, produced one *Major Matt Mason* book entitled "Moon Mission." We were introduced, in this book, to a number of new characters including *Captain Otto*

The rare *Major Matt Mason* wallet and binder

Part 2 - Major Matt Mason: Mattel's Man In Space

Major Matt Mason Space Exploration Game

Frame tray puzzle

Harvey and his sister, also an astronaut, *Jo Ann Harvey.* Perhaps this is where some collectors believe that they've seen a female *Major Matt Mason* astronaut. This book, incidentally, is one of the most common, if not the

most common *Major Matt Mason* item. It can easily be purchased for five to ten dollars. Whitman / Western Publishing also manufactured two puzzles, the first, a frame-tray puzzle, was a simple large-piece child's puzzle. As you can see, it's very colorful with an illustration of *Matt* riding his *Space Sled* across the barren lunar surface. The second puzzle produced by Whitman, which came in a beautiful box, roughly 8" x

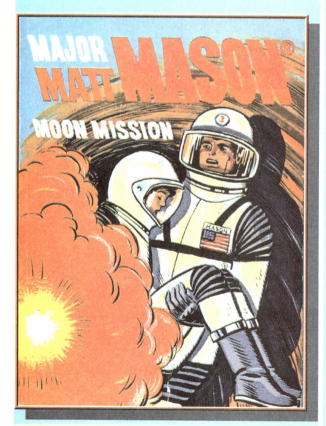

The Big Little series Moon Mission book featuring *Matt Mason*

Round puzzle

Part 2 - *Major Matt Mason*: Mattel's Man In Space

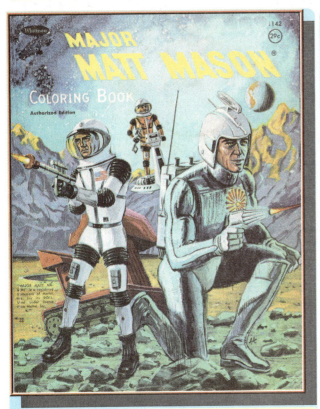

Major Matt Mason coloring book cover

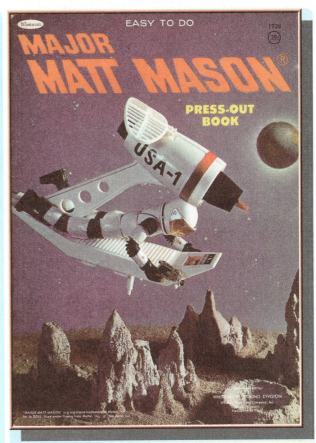

Major Matt Mason press-out book cover

10", is round, with excellent artwork of a *Firebolt Space Cannon* with *Sgt. Storm* on the lunar surface and *Major Matt Mason* controlling the vehicle. Aliens, who seem to be flying by way of futuristic power packs, appear to be attacking our brave astronauts. The lunar mountains watch silently in the foreground, with earth hanging in the eastern-most night sky. This particular puzzle was one in a series of "Junior Guild" puzzles and, at 125 pieces, was more complex than the *Space Sled Major Matt Mason* puzzle at 26 pieces. The *Major Matt Mason* coloring book and the press-out book were both items which depicted, by way of beautifully illustrated and colorful graphics, the *Man in Space* series. The coloring book's artistic cover shows the characters *Major Matt*, *Sgt. Storm* and *Captain Lazer*, who is the hero of the coloring book, fighting off aliens who appear to be attempting to take over the moon. Neither this

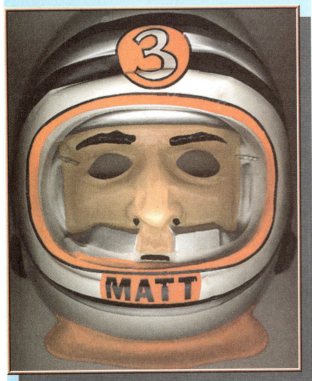

Major Matt Mason Halloween costume mask

Major Matt Mason Halloween costume

Part 2 - *Major Matt Mason*: Mattel's *Man In Space*

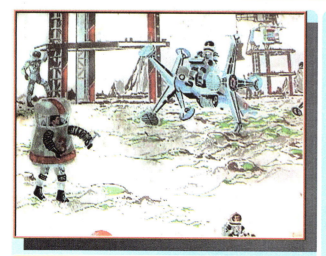

Very rare *Matt Mason* wallpaper

Major Matt is even chronicled in comic books

Matt Mason post card

coling book, nor the press-out *Matt Mason* book are commonplace today, and each can, if in good condition, command over one hundred dollars. The press-out book cover art is an illustration of *Matt Mason* flying his *Reconojet* over the moon's surface. The barren, crater scarred surface appears to be the color of sand, with a deep mauve sky. Turn the cover of this rare book and you'll find many Mattel *Man in Space* vehicles, astronauts and accessories. The centerfold is a lunarscape depicting cavernous mountains and, in the diamond-like night sky, a *Space Station*. The space ships and spaced-out vehicles found in the book can be slotted into respective openings, so that they appear to fly across the surface of the black velvet, diamond-strewn sky. Late in 1969, *Major Matt Mason* wallpaper was produced, as was a Collegeville Halloween Costume, recently sold through the Internet, both of which are scarce and rare finds.

Part 2 - *Major Matt Mason:* **Mattel's Man In Space**

Prototypes And The Rumor Mill

Among the things creating interest in the collecting field are those elusive prototype toys and rumors. I have denoted in this chapter the differences in colors and molding rumored to exist on many of the *Matt Mason* figures and vehicles. These rumors drive collectors to search for that special toy, like a Holy Grail, and Mattel Toys has certainly had their fair share of rumored products and strange prototypes. It's important to remember that any toy company will make many different models of a toy prior to finalizing the design that will be mass produced and ultimately stock the shelves of toy and hobby stores. I will review in this chapter items that you may or may not have seen which were slated for production, but, for many reasons, didn't make the cut and, as a result, didn't come to fruition. If you're a reader of the science fiction magazine *Starlog*, you may have seen the item pictured here. This toy looked somewhat like a *Reconojet* crossed with an *Astro Trac*. Like the *Reconojet*, the Mattel prototype pictured shows a large red flywheeled vehicle moving by way of a black support string. This toy didn't enter production.

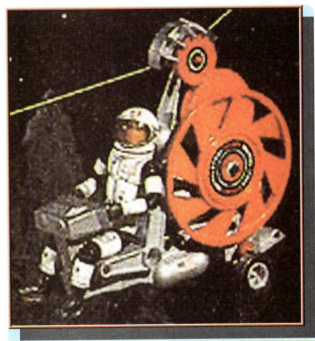

The prototype *Space Rover* which was never sold

Examine your *Space Station* box photographs and, if you're fortunate enough to have an early production box, you'll see that our favorite *Major* is wearing his knife belt, but, rather than carrying the produced knife, he has an non-produced gun in the holster. If you take an even closer look on the same *Space Station* box, you'll notice another accessory that wasn't produced — a flashlight. *Sgt. Storm* is thought, by some, to have been manufactured early on wearing a red space helmet. I've

heard rumors that the red color was unstable and chipped badly. Mattel Toys, having had many returned helmets and figures, quickly moved to producing all figures with white-only helmets. Some collectors support this speculation because *Sgt. Storm* is shown in some illustrations, for instance on the *Satellite Locker* box, wearing a red helmet. I personally haven't seen a red helmet, nor do I know of any collectors that currently have in their possession an original red helmet. I say an "original" since helmets, as with many other accessory items, are currently being reproduced and newly manufactured red helmets are available. *Captain Lazer* is shown in some early Mattel prototype photographs wearing a rather square white helmet and in the SEARS 1968 Christmas catalogue he's photographed with a significant variation — an open right hand, which should be holding his molded gun. Both of these *Captain Lazer* variations were not produced. If you're fortunate enough to own a *Major Matt Mason Moon Suit* card, you may notice that the bellows that are shown on the box photography are clear in color, unlike the produced yellow bellows. This can only be seen on early production boxes. Finally, the picture of the *Firebolt Space Cannon* is a prototype and, much like the *Space Station*, was initially made using different colors. The body of the *Cannon* is correct, being molded in white, however, the base, which was produced in a reddish / orange plastic, is shown as silver, as is the battery cover and the rotating space antennae.

Mattel's Astrospace Center Club

I would like to thank Larry Chinn for the information provided in this section. Without his help, the information and images would not be available. The *Major Matt Mason* Club was a product of the Mattel think tank. Little astronauts could join this club in 1967. By doing so, the new conscript would receive a package from the Mattel Toy company with the following items enclosed:

A white envelope with blue graphic of *Major Matt Mason*. This was the mailer envelope.

A signed photograph of an illustrated *Major Matt Mason* astronaut.

ASTRONAUT'S IDENTIFICATION CARD

has earned official Mattel astronaut rating and has demonstrated:

- courageous spirit in meeting the challenges of Space!
- ability to operate the Space Crawler, Jet Propulsion Pak and Space Sled
- dexterity to assemble and maintain the fully-equipped Space Station.

This astronaut is now a permanent member of the Mattel Space Community.

Major Matt Mason

Major MATT MASON

©1967 Mattel, Inc., Hawthorne, California
Printed in U.S.A.

A postage-sized blue and black collector's pin that could be worn by the new *Major Matt Mason* fan club member. The pin face was square and contained a blue oval background with the familiar *Matt Mason* figure and logo, dated 1966 Mattel.

Included in the envelope of goodies mailed to the new member was a *Major Matt Mason* identification card. This card identified the person carrying it as member of the space community.

Also included was membership card stating that the holder was "Declared flight-ready and awarded all M.A.C. privileges."

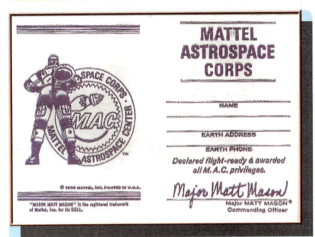

This package contained an iron-on patch that could be put on any cloth material or T-shirt. It was brightly colored showing a black and white *Matt Mason* logo. Note the red dots on the *Matt Mason* suit. M.A.C. was highlighted in red with the Astrospace Center writing highlighted in yellow.

Finally, also included in the envelope, was an order form for the *Major Matt Mason* child-sized M.A.C. baseball cap.

Morphing Major Matt Mason
And His Foreign Counterparts

Like the first beeps of the Soviet Union's own satellite, *Sputnik*, that were beamed around the world, so too was *Major Matt Mason* marketed worldwide. Many countries were able to receive the *Man in Space* toys by Mattel through either their subsidiaries or through a designated importer. Most of the *Major Matt Mason* product line was simply repacked, not withstanding the Latin American company CIPSA. CIPSA produced some toy accessories and figures after the *Major Matt Mason* line of toys had been discontinued in the United States. In this chapter, I'll discuss the variations that occurred with *Matt Mason* in different countries. Keep in mind that new *Major Matt Mason* color variations continue, to this date, to be found in countries as diverse as Africa and Canada.

CIPSA / Latin America

The CIPSA company was based in Mexico and appears to have made variations and taken liberties with the *Man in Space* line

of toys well after production ceased on the original Mattel toys. It would also appear that they acquired *Man in Space* molds and began producing remnants of the toy line. I have, in my personal collection, a number of *Major Matt Mason: Man in Space* toys manufactured by CIPSA. Compagnia Industrial de Plasticosm S.A. (CIPSA) changed not only the names of all the *Major Mason* characters, but also recast them in different colors, packaged them in different boxes, and changed their character / personality profiles.

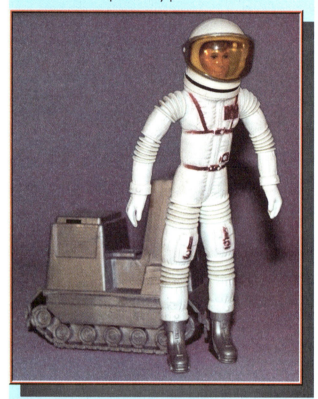

Capitan Meteoro - the Mexican Matt Mason

The new characters were now *Capitan Meteoro* (*Sgt. Storm*), who I own, molded in white rubber. This is not to be confused with the white rubber *Major Matt Mason* figures that were initially released by Mattel in

Atomo

Capitan Meteoro and the familiar Space Sled

1967. The *Capitan Meteoro / Sgt. Storm* figure's white rubber is not as pliable its American counterpart. The painted detailing on the figure is almost non-existent. The harness is painted only on the front and with a burgundy paint. The knee pads are painted a similar color, as is the flag, which is now a square block of paint without detail. *Capitan Meteoro* wears a white helmet and silver boots. There are variations in the actual molds, and not just in the detail painting. The ribbed

Capitan Meteoro's Cat Trac was molded in silver with no paint detailing

Part 2 - *Major Matt Mason*: Mattel's *Man In Space*

joints of *Capitan Meteoro* are thicker and have fewer ribs than the Mattel produced *Sgt. Storm* figure. A fellow collector has in his possession two different *Capitan Meteoros* — a yellow figure with blue painted boots and straps, and also a white figure with a black boots and silver helmet. I'm also aware of another white figure with matching white boots. The various paint changes reported for this figure would suggest that perhaps CIPSA utilized various colors of rubber and plastics, and we can thus expect more variations to come to light as *Major Matt Mason* and his various incarnations continue to gain momentum throughout the world. As of the printing of this book, a boxed *Capitan Meteoro* has not come to light. He is pictured in the CIPSA literature as sold with his *Cat / Lunar Trac*. Unlike the red and white *Cat Trac* produced for the Mattel line, *Capitan Meteoro*'s personal *Lunar Trac* was molded in silver. I've seen loose but complete figures selling for as much as $150.00, as much or more than a loose *Jeff Long* figure.

One other figure manufactured by CIPSA was *Callisto*. He was renamed *Cripton* for this Spanish line and is not an alien friend to *Major Matt Mason*, but instead is the *Major's* evil arch enemy. *Cripton* is most notable because he was molded in an almost translucent green rubber. Like *Meteoro*, he has little detail painting, with blue boots, blue suit details and fiery orange eyes being the exception. He was sold, as was the original *Callisto*, with his *Space Sensor* and *Bellow*, this time molded in a deep blood red color. His box was very colorful, depicting a Mattel photograph of *Callisto*, with his sensor, standing on an orange alien surface. Inside this box, the CIPSA color variation came with no inserts, but included Spanish instructions. From a dealer, one can expect to pay $200.00 for a good condition figure and box.

Cripton and his accessories came loose in a box

The final character in the CIPSA line of toys was *Scorpio el Tirano*. He was the "tyrant" according to CIPSA. *Scorpio* was marketed in a very bright pink box. He is notable in that there appears to be a number of color

Cripton was *Callisto's* Mexican name

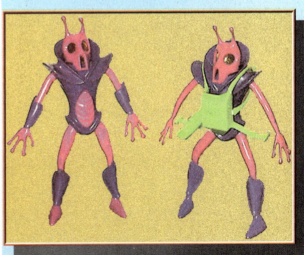

CIPSA's *Scorpio el Tirano* versus Mattel's *Scorpio*

SCORPIO
¡El Tirano!

Enemigo
intergaláctico del
Capitán Meteoro..

Cuando
Scorpio ataca,
sus ojos
se prenden
y se apagan
furiosamente.

Scorpio El Tirano was sold loose in a box

variations — pink bodies, purple feet and guards, pink feet and pink guards, and any combination of these. The shading of pink appears to change from time to time between figures as well. *Tirano* is also notable in that his

Scorpio El Tirano - same mold as the original, but different colors

glowing yellow speckled dome is of a different color shading of plastic composite with a different gold flake. He was not sold with his vest projector and, like *Cripton*, was loose in his box. You shouldn't pay more than $200.00 currently for this figure, since he, like *Cripton*, is readily available.

EXTENSOR DE PODER

Equipo espacial para librar peligrosos obstáculos en planetas hostiles.

Mexican Power-Limbs for that big enchilada

CIPSA's continuing product line of the defunked *Man in Space* toys includes the *Capsula Cosmica* (*Space Power Suit*), *Extensor de Poder* (*Supernaut Power Limbs*), *Canon Espacial* (*Firebolt Space Cannon*), *Camara Antigravedad* (*Uni-Tred Space Hauler and Space Bubble*) and *Estacion Espacial* (*Space Station.*) The *Space Station* is notable for a number of reasons. There have been rumors for a very long time of an "alien space station." This would most certainly be that station. Rather than graphics for the command center showing *Major Matt Mason* on the computer screens (remember he didn't exist in the CIPSA world of *Capitan Meteoro*), they show *Scorpio el*

Cañón Espacial

CIPSA's Firebolt Space Cannon

Part 2 - *Major Matt Mason:* Mattel's *Man In Space*

Cámara Antigravedad

Mexican *Space Bubble* and *Space Station*

Estación Espacial

definite red not an orange color (as per Mattel), and most significantly, as it dates this toy as an early 1970's production, the beacon is molded in white plastic and has six fins. It would appear that this toy utilized the same mold as the Mattel *Space 1999* vinyl play set command center, produced circa 1974.

Rosebud Mattel / United Kingdom

Rosebud was the UK marketing arm for Mattel Inc. Toymakers, Hawthorne, California. It would appear that, for some of the *Major Matt Mason* items, Rosebud Mattel was responsible for importing the toy line. No variations have been found in the toys themselves, with all toys having been made in Hong Kong as were their American counterparts. Variations of the line are limited to the Rosebud Mattel logo being used on the exterior of some, but not all, of the packaging. Other variations included a few accessory name changes, for example the *Firebolt Space Cannon* was renamed the *Firebolt Space Lazer* and *Major Matt Mason*'s name was abbreviated to *Matt Mason*. As for packaging changes, wording, where applicable, was changed from American standard to Oxford text. These changes were inclusive to not only the exterior box wording, but to instruction sheets as well. For ease of identification of Rosebud Mattel, simply check the exterior box to see where the box was printed. Rosebud will be identified as "printed in England."

Mattel spA / Italy

It would appear that the *Major Matt Mason* line of toys was imported to Italy beginning about one year later (1968) than when it was released in the United States and Canada. The catalogue

Tirano. The *Space Station* has a number of color variations from its American counterpart — the dark blue Mattel station panels contrast sharply with the very light blue *Estacion Espacial* panels, the girders are a

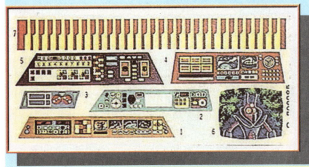

The Mexican (a.k.a. Alien) *Space Station* decals

Major Matt Mason repackaged and translated into Italian

numbers, as with the UK numbers, correspond to the US factory stock lists. The box and instruction text was translated from English to Italian. Due to the inability to always make direct translations, *Matt Mason* item names were not always exact. For example, the *Space Crawler* was referred to as the *Rotoragna* (rotary spider.) All Italian boxed *Matt Mason* items carried the Mattel spA logo on box and toy instruction artwork.

Mattel GmbH Spielzeug

Mattel GmbH was the importer to Germany, Switzerland and Austria of *Major Matt Mason* items. As with the Italian toys, they arrived in Europe in 1968. All Mattel GmbH *Matt Mason* toys received repackaging and translation of text from their US toy counterparts. Again, exact translations were not always possible. For instance, the *Space Bubble* was referred to as the *Space-ball* on all box artwork and instruction sheets. There were no known German-only toys manufactured.

German *Power Suit* and *Reconojet*

German *Power-Limbs*

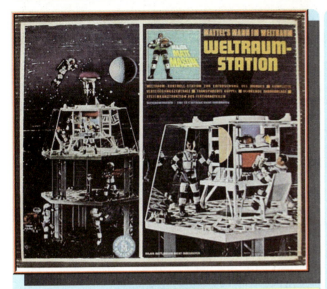

German *Space Station*

The Canadian-only *Astro Trac Gift Set* and a French Canadian *Matt Mason*

Mattel / Canadian and French-Canada

As described earlier in this book, the Canadian market did get a boxed *Major Matt Mason* item that wasn't available in the United States of America and elsewhere worldwide with the exception of the SEARS department store exclusive *Astro Trac Gift Set*. All Canadian box artwork has white bordering on exterior box graphics, whereas US box artwork is black bordered. The French-Canadian box wording was translated from the English language versions, but did make a few alterations. The French translations replaced the word astronaut with cosmonaut (Russian for astronaut, a strange combination of languages.) Most times, French-Canadian translations were printed on stickers that were placed over the English descriptions. Some packaging had both English and French titles and descriptions printed directly on the box and instruction sheet. When this was the case, the box would show the English as the primary text and the French translations would usually be in small print below. There were times when instruction sheets were mixed and a French-Canadian boxed item was packaged with an English-only instruction sheet or vise versa.

Major Matt Mason Price Guide And Values

Regardless of what my publisher and I may think of price guides, in and of themselves, we agree that they help to sell books, and that we are both in favor of selling books, so a price guide has been included here. I'm sure that you'll find this guide controversial, and at times will disagree with prices given. I hope, as well, that you'll find pricing that pleases you in this guide. In an area such as *Major Matt Mason*, which has seen a tremendous growth in collectability over the last few years, prices are rising very rapidly. The prices in this guide were as accurate as possible at the time of going to press, but things move so fast that you may find that variations have taken place in the months it has taken for the book to be produced. The *Major Matt Mason* toy values presented in this reference guide are based on years of collecting and speaking with numerous collectors and dealers worldwide, as well as what I, myself, have paid for a particular toy. The prices that are shown reflect the 1998-99 prices that you can expect to pay for a Mattel *Major Matt Mason* toy and/or accessory. Further, the values are based on dealer asking prices at toy shows, in printed sources such as toy collectable publications and mail order, through Internet dealers, and at auction web sites. Also, prices are in part, frankly, based on guesswork. This is not to imply that the price paid for a particular toy is the actual value of the toy. As with any collectable item, the value is directly related to the intrinsic value that a prospective collector places on the item. This is particularly true of a rare toy or variation, since the item in question is as valuable to the collector as what he or she is willing to pay, and the published value of the toy becomes unimportant. It's important to note however that rarity doesn't always equate to value. Within the collecting field, a collector wishing to obtain items of special interest often generates the strongest demand. Rarity is only part of the value of the toy. It should also be noted that from region to region and country to country toy prices do fluctuate. Prices will be significantly higher for a collectable toy that is found in New York City, Los Angeles or Toronto, Canada than in, for instance, Pennsylvania or Ohio which have some of the lowest pricing of collectable toys in the United States. Yes, there will be times when you stumble across a toy which should command high prices in the marketplace, but is priced low — there was the time that I have stumbled across a *Jeff Long* Mattel *Man in Space* toy, complete and in excellent condition with an asking price of $10.00. I have also paid $150.00 for a similar figure. This must be kept in mind when reviewing the various collector books. Supply and demand is most often the determining factor for pricing any collectable toy, along with the second most important price determining factor, complete and original boxes, packaging and instructions. In some situations, and specifically with *Major Matt Mason* toys, the box artwork can be more interesting and attractive than the toys themselves. The value of the loose toy can dramatically increase when boxed. Toy catalogues and original box packing, when present, will again add to the asking price. I suspect that there are many household basements, attics and old toy store stock rooms just waiting to be discovered that will bring more *Major Matt Mason* into the marketplace. In fact, I had one such experience myself. While away for the weekend in a small fishing village in Southern Ontario, Canada, I happened to be in an old bowling alley with a few friends. While bowling, I noticed two boxes labeled Mattel in the rafters above our heads. After speaking with the owner for a few minutes, I was able to convince him to locate a ladder for me so that I could check them out. To my surprise, when I got both boxes down from the rafters and opened them, I found complete and unopened *Power Limbs* and *Space Power Suits*, still mint on their cards. The owner, happy to be rid of that "old junk in the rafters" charged me the original going price for the *Power Limbs* back in the late 1960's — a dollar per item. Needless to say, I bought

both boxes! From time to time, small pockets of warehouse finds really do occur, bringing toys into the collector's arena and, most often, reducing the value of the toy found for a period of time. This guide will include two prices for each item. The first price will be for a loose item, such as, a toy accessory or *Major Matt Mason* "bendie" figure. When the item is described as loose, I'm referring to an item that is not boxed or carded, but is complete. The second price provided will be for a boxed or carded toy in mint / like new condition. It should be noted that if a toy box or card is torn, worn or missing end flaps, or doesn't have its inner packing or decals, it is neither complete nor mint and, in the real world, shouldn't demand the maximum price for the toy, but rather should fall into the price range between a loose and boxed item. It truly is at the discretion of the buyer, and the willingness of the seller, to arrange an agreeable amount for a particular toy item. There are some *Major Matt Mason* items that are more rare than others because of color variations. A white molded *Major Matt Mason* figure is more rare, and therefore more sought after and higher priced than a comparable black rubber, white painted *Major Matt Mason* figure. These variations will be denoted in the price guide as well for your information. The prices that I've provided in this reference guide are the prices that you should expect to pay to buy an item. They are not necessarily what you can expect to receive when you are selling the same toy to a toy dealer. In fact, you should expect about fifty percent of the guide price when selling to a dealer. Finally, the prices provided here are based on United States currency.

How to use this *Major Matt Mason*: Mattel's *Man in Space* Reference Guide:

The following pages are itemized by toy using the original Mattel stock numbers for the *Major Matt Mason* toy line. The stock numbers are followed by the toy figure or accessory name, the Mint Value of the loose toy, and/or the MIB (mint in box) value of the toy. The MIB designation actually represents MOC (mint on card) for some items. You'll note that most toys have a value for both the Mint Value and the MIB Value. There are times however, when a toy may have a N/A under the Mint Value heading. I have compiled the list this way so a toy either off its card or out of its box can be calculated separately. There are prices for toys that were not originally sold separately at the end of the chapter, including; astronaut figures, *Cat Tracs*, *Jet Propulsion Paks*, *Space Sleds* and so forth.

Part 2 - *Major Matt Mason*: Mattel's *Man In Space*

Major Matt Mason: Mattel's Man In Space 1967 - 1970

Stock Number: 5157
Item Name: **Talking Command Console**
Mint Value: 45.00
MIB Value: 120.00
Description:
"Mattel's First Talking Space Toy." This black strapped carrying case / play station was a "talkie", speaking ten different phrases.

Stock Number: 6300
Item Name: **Major Matt Mason Flight Pak**
Mint Value: N/A
MIB Value: 400.00
Description:
A white *Major Matt Mason* toy figure, helmet, two-piece *Space Sled*, *Jet Propulsion Backpack* and *Space Sled* decal sheet.

Stock Number: 6301
Item Name: **Moon Suit Pak**
Mint Value: 35.00
MIB Value: 155.00
Description:
A molded white plastic dome-type suit with attached accordion flexible rubber arms.

Stock Number: 6302
Item Name: **Astro Trac**
Mint Value: 55.00
MIB Value: 200.00
Description:
A white plastic battery powered one man "mobile explorer."

Stock Number: 6303
Item Name: **Matt Mason with Moon Suit**
Mint Value: N/A
MIB Value: 550.00
Description:
A *Matt Mason* figure with *Moon Suit* and accessories.

Stock Number: 6304
Item Name: **Space Crawler**
Mint Value: 20.00
MIB Value: 125.00
Description:
This "invincible" vehicle tracks over the roughest terrain and always lands on its legs.

Stock Number: 6305
Item Name: **Rocket Launch Pak**
Mint Value: 25.00

MIB Value: 75.00
Description:
A defense weapon, remote controlled rocket *Launcher*.

Rocket Launcher and the *Rotogun* included in the *Rocket Launch Pak*

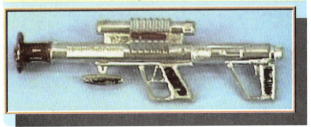

Stock Number: 6306
Item Name: **Satellite Launch Pak**
Mint Value: 25.00
MIB Value: 75.00
Description:
A *Launcher* with four "*communication satellites.*"

Stock Number: 6307
Item Name: **Space Probe Pak**
Mint Value: 25.00
MIB Value: 75.00
Description:
A silver molded, remote control launch base and turret, binoculars and flare gun.

Stock Number: 6308
Item Name: **Space Station**
Mint Value: 50.00
MIB Value: 275.00
Description:
The *Space Station* is a highly detailed set. Many parts are often missing.

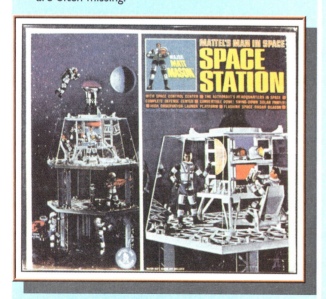

Stock Number: 6310
Item Name: **Space Station Crawler Deluxe Action Set**
Mint Value: N/A
MIB Value: 300.00
Description:
The *Space Station Crawler Deluxe Action Set* was the first toy packaged by the Mattel company for the Mattel *Man in Space* line.

Stock Number: 6311
Item Name: **Space Crawler Action Set**
Mint Value: N/A
MIB Value: 400.00
Description:
This set included *Major Matt Mason*, a *Space Sled*, the *Crawler*, and a *Jet Pack*.

Stock Number: 3616
Item Name: **Matt Mason Space Ship Case**
Mint Value: N/A
MIB Value: 200.00
Description:
This *Rocket Ship Carrying Case* was manufactured to "hold *Matt Mason*."

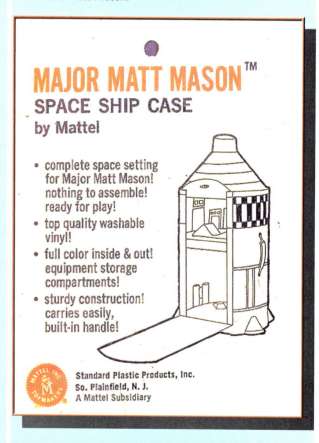

Part 2 - *Major Matt Mason:* Mattel's *Man In Space*

Stock Number: 3617
Item Name: **Sgt. Storm Flight Pak**
Mint Value: N/A
MIB Value: 600.00
Description:
Sgt. Storm was sold with either his *Flight Pak Set* or with his *Cat Trac*.

Stock Number: 6318
Item Name: **Matt Mason with Cat Trac**
Mint Value: N/A
MIB Value: 400.00
Description:
Matt was sold sitting atop a red *Cat Trac*.

Stock Number: 6319
Item Name: **Sgt. Storm with Cat Trac**
Mint Value: N/A
MIB Value: 500.00
Description:
Sgt. Storm was packaged sitting atop his white *Cat Trac*.

Stock Number: 6320
Item Name: **Reconojet Pak**
Mint Value: 25.00
MIB Value: 75.00
Description:
The *Reconojet* was a white molded, string operated vehicle.

Stock Number: 6321
Item Name: **Space Shelter Pak**
Mint Value: 25.00
MIB Value: 75.00
Description:
This pak included the inflator pump and tent, plus accessories.

Stock Number: 6322
Item Name: **Satellite Locker**
Mint Value: 20.00
MIB Value: 65.00
Description:
This was a storage locker for *Major Matt*.

Stock Number: 6327
Item Name: **Astro Trac Missile Convoy Set**
Mint Value: N/A
MIB Value: 1200.00
Description:
This toy was sold only through SEARS.

Part 2 - Major Matt Mason: Mattel's *Man In Space*

Vinyl lunarscape and craters from the *Astro Trac Missile Convoy Set*

Stock Number: 6328
Item Name: *Mobile Launch Pad*
Mint Value: 100.00
MIB Value: 170.00
Description:
   This item was sold through SEARS only.

Stock Number: 6330
Item Name: *Captain Laser*
Mint Value: N/A
MIB Value: 150.00
Description:
   This toy was billed as "*Major Matt Mason*'s friend from Outer Space."

Stock Number: 6331
Item Name: *Callisto*
Mint Value: N/A
MIB Value: 225.00
Description:
   Callisto was the mysterious alien from Jupiter.

Stock Number: 6332
Item Name: *Jeff Long - Space Scientist Rocketry*
Mint Value: N/A
MIB Value: 650.00

Description:
   Jeff Long was the black American Astronaut produced for the Mattel's *Major Matt Mason* line of toys.

Stock Number: 6333
Item Name: *Doug Davis Space Scientist*
Mint Value: N/A
MIB Value: 450.00
Description:
   This yellow astronaut was the Radiologist sitting atop his *Cat Trac*.

Stock Number: 6336
Item Name: *Major Matt Mason and Space Power Suit*
Mint Value: N/A
MIB Value: 450.00
Description:
   Matt Mason came carded with the *Space Power Suit*.

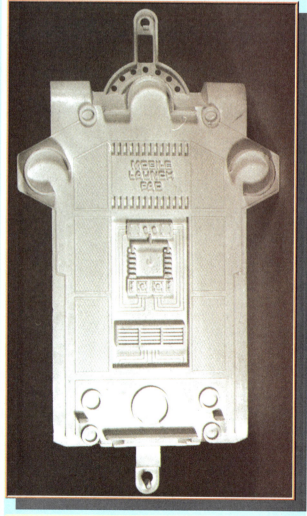

Mobile Launch Pad

Part 2 - *Major Matt Mason*: Mattel's *Man In Space*

Stock Number: 6337
Item Name: **Space Mission Team**
Mint Value: N/A
MIB Value: 600.00
Description:
 This set came in a photo box displaying the figures of *Major Matt* and his buddies.

Stock Number: 6339
Item Name: **Uni-Tred and Space Bubble**
Mint Value: N/A
MIB Value: 100.00
Description:
 This large box came with a front graphic displaying the red *Uni-Tred* pulling the *Space Bubble*.

Stock Number: 6340
Item Name: **Firebolt Space Cannon**
Mint Value: 30.00
MIB Value: 125.00
Description:
 This box included the *Space Cannon*, a large battery operated toy with both lights and sound.

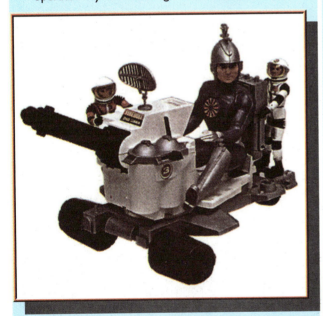

Stock Number: 6341
Item Name: **Firebolt Space Cannon**
                  Super Action Set
Mint Value: N/A
MIB Value: 375.00
Description:
 This set came in a large picture box and included the figures *Major Matt Mason*, *Sgt. Storm*, and *Captain Lazer* sold together with the *Firebolt Space Cannon*.

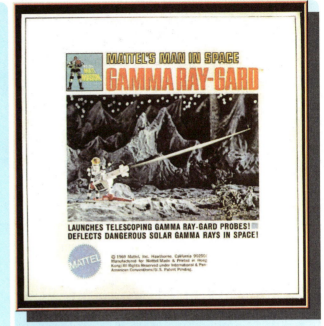

Stock Number: 6342
Item Name: **Gamma Ray Gard Pak**
Mint Value: 15.00
MIB Value: 100.00
Description:
 The *Gamma Ray Gard* was a missile firing defense system.

Stock Number: 6343
Item Name: **Supernaut Power Limbs Pak**
Mint Value: 20.00
MIB Value: 75.00
Description:
 Before *Ripley's Alien* fighter, there was *Matt's* Power Limbs.

Part 2 - *Major Matt Mason*: Mattel's *Man In Space*

Stock Number: 6344
Item Name: **Space Power Suit Pak**
Mint Value: 20.00
MIB Value: 75.00
Description:
   The *Power Suit Pak* protects *Major Matt* from the hazards of interstellar space.

Stock Number: 6345
Item Name: **Space Bubble**
Mint Value: 20.00
MIB Value: 90.00
Description:
   The *Space Bubble* is a 7" diameter ball with a gyro-command seat.

Stock Number: 6346
Item Name: **Uni-Tred Space Hauler**
Mint Value: 40.00
MIB Value: 95.00
Description:
   This red molded plastic vehicle could climb just about any mountainous terrain.

Stock Number: 6347
Item Name: **Space Travel Pak**
Mint Value: 35.00
MIB Value: 75.00
Description:
   The *Space Sled* and *Jet Propulsion Pack* rounded on this carded set.

Stock Number: 6351
Item Name: **Firebolt Space Cannon Action Set with Captain Lazer**
Mint Value: N/A
MIB Value: 295.00
Description:
   The *Firebolt Space Cannon Action Set* included not only the *Space Cannon*, but also the figure *Captain Lazer*.

Stock Number: 6353
Item Name: **Lunar Base Command Set**
Mint Value: N/A
MIB Value: 800.00
Description:
   The *Lunar Base Set* is the largest box set of the Mattel's *Man in Space* series of toys.

Stock Number: 6355
Item Name: **Space Discovery Set**
Mint Value: N/A
MIB Value: 625.00
Description:
   The *Space Discovery Set* includes *Callisto*, *Doug Davis* with his *Cat Trac*, *Space Crawler*, *Space Bubble* and *Space Power Suit*.

Stock Number: 6356
Item Name: **Orbitor with Or**
Mint Value: N/A
MIB Value: N/A
Description:
   Or is not known to have been produced.

Stock Number: 6357
Item Name: **Star Seeker with Memory Guidance System**
Mint Value: 25.00
MIB Value: 135.00
Description:
   The *Star Seeker* capsule was a D-size battery operated white space ship.

Stock Number: 6359
Item Name: **Scorpio**
Mint Value: 350.00
MIB Value: 800.00

Part 2 - Major Matt Mason: Mattel's *Man In Space*

Description:

Scorpio was the final *Man in Space* figure marketed by Mattel.

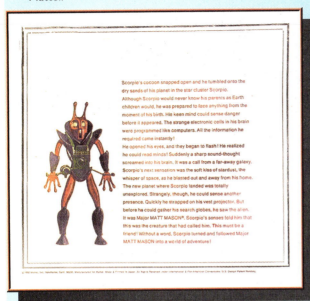

Back of the *Scorpio* box describing his origin

Stock Number: 6360
Item Name: **XRG-1 Reentry Glider**
Mint Value: 175.00
MIB Value: 400.00
Description:

This *Glider* was the equivalent of the NASA space shuttle for *Major Matt Mason*, his buddies and *Callisto*.

Stock Number: 6361
Item Name: **XRG-1 Reentry Glider
                with Major Matt Mason**
Mint Value: N/A
MIB Value: 550.00
Description:

This *Major Matt Mason* toy includes the *Reentry Glider* and white *Matt* figure.

Stock Number: 6362
Item Name: **Talking Major Matt Mason**
Mint Value: N/A
MIB Value: 350.00
Description:

The talking *Major Matt Mason* pack came with the standard issue white *Major Matt* figure plus the *Talking Backpack*.

Stock Number: 6378
Item Name: **Talking Major Matt Mason
                with XRG-1 Reentry Glider**
Mint Value: N/A
MIB Value: 650.00

Description:

This pack included number 6362 (*Major Matt Mason* with *Talking Back Pack*) and the *Reentry Glider*.

Stock Number: 6379
Item Name: **Major Matt Mason
                Super Power Equipment Set**
Mint Value: N/A
MIB Value: 300.00
Description:

Included in this "Super Set" was *Major Matt Mason*, *Power Limbs*, red *Cat Trac* and *Space Power Suit*.

Stock Number: 6380
Item Name: **Voyage to Galaxy III Set**
Mint Value: N/A
MIB Value: N/A
Description:

This set is not known to exist.

Stock Number: 6386
Item Name: **Star Seeker Walk in Space Set**
Mint Value: N/A
MIB Value: 1000.00
Description:

This boxed set included both the *Star Seeker* and a *Major Matt Mason* figure.

Stock Number: 8178
Item Name: **Astro Trac Gift Set**
Mint Value: N/A
MIB Value: 1400.00
Description:

This boxed set included both the *Sgt. Storm* and *Major Matt Mason* figures, and one *Mobile Launch Pad* with a *Satellite Launcher*.

Part 2 - *Major Matt Mason*: Mattel's *Man In Space*

Stock Number: 8874
Item Name: **Astronaut individually boxed**
Mint Value: N/A
MIB Value: 225.00
Description:

This boxed generic *Major Matt Mason* figure was sold at, among other space installations, NASA's Cape Canaveral in Cocoa Beach Florida.

Individual Loose Toy Figures And Accessories

Some toys were never sold as individual items. These toys most often were sold on a card with a number of other toys and accessories. The prices below are for loose toys and accessories in mint condition.

Space Sled	15.00
Cat Trac / Lunar Trac	15.00
Jet Propulsion Pak	30.00
Talking Back Pack	35.00
Helmet and visor	25.00
Chrome tools	5.00
Chrome weapons	5.00
Gard projectiles	10.00
Mini catalogues	25.00
Callisto harness	30.00
Scorpio harness	50.00

As with the accessory toys, the astronauts will be found, more often than not, off of their respective cards and loose with no accessories, except perhaps their helmets. Therefore, I've priced the astronauts individually. The price associated with each astronaut is for a mint condition figure. That is, by definition, a figure that has little or no paint wear and no broken wires. The prices reflect a figure that is complete with the helmet and visor. As with all toys priced here, the figure value will decrease in direct proportion to poor paint, broken wires, melt marks, a missing helmet, and general wear and tear.

Matt Mason & helmet	55.00
Matt Mason white rubber	75.00
Sgt. Storm	60.00
Doug Davis	70.00
Jeff Long	125.00
Callisto	65.00
Captain Lazer	75.00
Scorpio	150.00

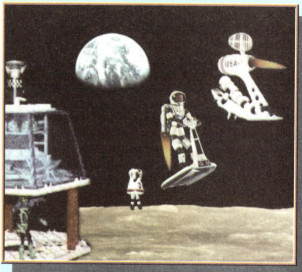

Ideal Toys
MIGHTY ZEROID ROBOTS
and
STAR TEAM

Zeroid Robots And The STAR Team (Ideal Toys)

ZEROIDS - Ideal's Work Horses Of The Future!

The Ideal Toy Company was a very innovative organization. Their slogan was "It's a wonderful toy, It's Ideal."

Ideal's humble beginnings go back to just after the turn of the century when Mr. Morris Michtem, in 1907, founded the company. The struggling corporation received a much needed boost when American President Teddy Roosevelt agreed to allow his name to be used on a small stuffed bear that the company had produced. It's amazing how one small act can change the history of a company. The "Teddy Bear" went on to establish Ideal as a leader in the market for female dolls and incredible 1960's toys. Many of the great toys of that decade, which are now highly collectable and sought after, can be attributed to toy designer Marvin Glass and his staff. Among those fantastic 1960's toys were the *Zeroid Robots*, believed by many to be the most inventive plastic robots to come out of the 60's.

Being a collector of *Zeroid* robots myself, I'd have to agree. The 1960's saw tremendous growth in television, advertising and toy company marketing. The space race between the United States and the Soviet Union had ignited the world, and science fiction and fantasy television interest was at an all time high. The Viet Nam war was raging, and rioting and anarchy were common on the local evening news. The toy industry reflected the public's concern, frustration and unrest — sales in previous toy strongholds were diminishing. I am, of course, referring to the decline of wartime action toys and figures.

Live action television shows, such as *The Time Tunnel*, *Star Trek*, *Voyage To The Bottom Of The Sea* and *Land Of The Giants* had hit a cord with the North American public. The live action television show *Lost In Space* first aired in 1965, and was an instant hit, as was *Batman* in 1966. It's hard to believe now, that this cult classic started life as a mid-season television replacement. *Lost In Space* was one of the first science fiction shows to be heavily licensed by the toy industry and went on to produce a multitude of spin-off toys and games, including none other than our most beloved "Robot." It too became a cult classic, as *Batman* did a year later, Which also spawned the 90's feature film.

Children's shows had also become involved in science fiction and fantasy with the likes of *Fireball XL5* and *Johnny Quest. Space Ghost* premiered in 1967, as did the animated series *Birdman*, which began to take interest and sales away from the established super hero toy favorites *Aquaman* and *Superman*. Science Fiction B-movies, like *Forbidden Planet*, were all the rage at the local drive-in theater. We also shouldn't forget that *2001 – A Space Odyssey* was just around the corner. Toy companies, targeting the post war "baby boomers" and their newly acquired affluence, were quick to use television as an advertising medium of great power and profitability. Television was still in its infancy, and was, of course, the best way to attract the interest of children to toys through inventive advertising.

Sandwiched between Science Fiction and Fantasy live action shows and cartoons were commercial after commercial about toys. *Billy Blastoff* by Eldon, Marx's *Big Loo* and *Moon Robot, Johnny Apollo*, Colorform's *Outer Space Men*, and the *Moon McDare* astronaut figure by Gilbert had collectively hit the toy buying public like a ton of bricks. Marx made the *Moon Robot* in 1962. He was over three feet tall. *Big Loo* was able to complete twelve mechanical operations, including firing ping-pong balls. The *Robot Commando*, made by Ideal Toys, was another famous and treasured robot. This 1961 Ideal creation was made of plastic molded in blue with red accents. He stood a sturdy 15" in height, and among his many features were rotating eyeballs, ball firing arms, and a missile firing head. On the other end of the size spectrum was *Billy Blastoff*. Little *Billy* and his accessories were tiny in comparison to *Big Loo*. *Billy* and his sidekick robot stood just over 4" in height. This hard plastic jointed action figure came with a myriad of accessories, including his *jet pack, space car, sled* and very *Major Matt Mason*-looking micro-sized *lunar crawler*.

The Colorform Company, seizing on the popularity of both *Major Matt Mason* and *Zeroid Robots*, jumped onto the bandwagon in 1968. Colorform released bendable rubber alien figures. These very strange looking figures ranged in size from tiny Alpha 7, standing 3" in height, to a 7" Colossus Rex — the Man from Jupiter. One of the most popular toys released in 1968 was the *Mighty Zeroid Robot* line manufactured by Ideal Toys.

The Ideal Toy Company had an earlier positive experience prior to creating their most famous robot line. They had produced the now classic *Mr. Machine* and *King-Zor* in the early half of the decade. Now the Ideal Toy Company, with impeccable timing, entered the space race and provided another series of toys that would compliment Mattel's *Major Matt Mason*.

By this time, Remco had also entered robot production with their *Lost In Space* "Robot". But *Zeroids* were perfect companions for *Major Matt Mason*, standing about an inch taller at 6½" to 7" in height. Physically and visually, they fit with *Major Matt Mason* and his accessories, resulting in enhanced play value, and in increased profitability for both toy companies. The eve of Christmas 1967 saw *Zeroids* sitting under many a child's Christmas tree. In fact, many boys, including myself, received both *Zeroids* and *Major Matt* from Santa Claus that year.

Standing tall and each looking every bit the menacing robot, *Zintar, Zerak* and *Zobor* looked like they could conquer any alien world. They possessed special mechanical enhancements that would allow the terraforming of many new worlds in far off solar systems. With NASA's space program in full swing, colonization of the stars seemed plausible, and not just grist for science fiction authors and television producers. Could mankind's future be hanging in the balance? Would "real" robots, like our *Zeroid* toys, be working with the brave men and women of the space program forging ahead into the deep reaches of outer space? *Major Matt Mason* and *Zeroid Robots* brought the future into focus for many a child, and this future did, for a time, seem real. Fantasy faded away to reality when Ideal suffered a number of disappointing losses in the early 1970's. *Zeroids'* popularity began to wane. Space travel had become almost routine and was no longer interesting to the general public.

The STAR TEAM accessory line of *Space Exploration Gear* was a failure, lasting just short of a year. *Star Wars* ignited sales of the STAR TEAM / *Zeroid* toys in the late 1970's, but it was too little too late. Ideal Toys was sold to CBS in the early 1980's, and a short time after was auctioned off to the highest bidder. ViewMaster, Hasbro and Milton Bradley all purchased pieces of this once powerful company. Luckily for us, the legacy of Ideal Toys — and it's slogan "It's a wonderful toy, It's Ideal" — lives on through it's imaginative toy line and those *motorific* powered *Zeroids*.

Mighty *Zeroids Robots* And Their Cosmic Accessories

This chapter will explore both non-mechanical and the mechanical operation of all Ideal *Zeroid Robots* and STAR TEAM toys. As with *Major Matt Mason*, *Zeroids* are often, after thirty years of sitting in household basements and attics, found incomplete, missing both packaging and accessories. This being the case, back board instructions are usually missing, since they were either part of a header card or a small slip of paper in a card box. I will, in this section, describe the action of all toys and accessory items, both non-mechanical and mechanical.

"Moving across the landscape, overrunning all obstacles as inexorable as the Future itself, these amazing, efficient and powerful automatons have but one purpose — serve their masters at work and play!"

Zeroids: Ideal Toys 1967 – 1970

| Zintar | Zerak | Zobor | Zemo |

The *Zeroid Robots*, *Zintar the (Silver) Explorer*, *Zerak the (Blue) Destroyer*, and *Zobor the (Bronze) Transporter*, all were designed with the same mechanical functions. All three robots came packaged with interchangeable "hands." These hands consisted of fist-like grips, lobster-like manually adjustable claws, a small magnetic hand, and a scope hand. These hands, when plugged into their respective wrist sockets on either wrist, would shoot the "*laser bombs*" that were packaged with *Zintar*, *Zerak* and *Zobor*. All robots were designed with a "chopping" action arm. The chopping action could be easily activated by first rotating the right arm until a click was heard. The arm would then be locked into position. The left arm simply needed to be rotated up and then pulled down. The "karate" arm would then chop down, shooting the "*lazer bomb*" out of its scooped hand.

Ideal advertised their *Zeroids* as each having a "unique

pair of special purpose hands, interchangeable magnetic and a throwing hands, and battery-powered motor with forward and reverse drive." *Zeroids*, it was advertised, "were capable of grabbing, pinching, carrying, clawing, attracting, throwing, pushing, pulling, or hauling functions."

Zeroids quickly zipped across polished kitchen floors, powered by their *motorific* motors located in their base and drawing energy from two AA-sized batteries. Take it from experience, don't try and run *Zeroids* across that thick shag carpeting. *Zintar*, *Zerak* and *Zobor* may have been billed as "Mighty" by Ideal Toys, but only a sharp pair of scissors would free their little axles and black rubberized tank-like treads from the strangle hold of "the incredible shag monster." "From Turret to track, each *Zeroid* simulates a marvelous mechano-electronic complex", it was said. Simply pop in two batteries that were concealed in the lower "leg" area of each robot, and flip the toggle switch at the rear base of the robot, and watch them go. *Zeroids* were pretty speedy and would race at high speed in either forward or reverse motion with a flip of a switch. Each *Zeroid* was supplied with a yellow *Zeroid* ramp. As the *Zeroid* approached the ramp, a small switch located underneath the robot would be switched and the *Zeroid* would reverse direction automatically.

Commander Zogg

Commander Zogg was the most unique *Zeroid*. He possessed more complex operations than his *Zeroid* cousins. *Zogg* was initially sold in a large elaborate playset named the *Zeroid Commander Action Playset*. I'll be discussing this set as an accessory item in a later section. As for *Zogg* and his actions, the similarities with his *Zeroid* cousins was that he too made use of two AA-size batteries to power his *motorific* power plant. His engine, as with *Zintar*, *Zerak* and *Zobor*, enabled him to move both forward and reverse with a flip of a switch. This is where the similarities ended however. *Zogg* didn't have interchangeable hands as the others did. He didn't have karate chopping arms either. What he could do, though, was light up and blink. He also, and more importantly, was able to power the accessories that were included in his action set. This was accomplished by *Zogg's* "electro / magnetic hands." Those two AA-size batteries were put to real use by this fellow, powering not only the *motorific* engine and torso light, but also

running an electrical current to the metal pads of *Zogg's* hands. When *Zogg* came into contact with the special electrical conduits of his accessories, they would scream and whirl to life with super charged power. *Zogg with his Laser Beam*, product number 4763-9, was advertised in the 1970 dealer catalogue on page 24 with the following description: "*Zogg*, the number one motorized *Zeroid* of them all is now available with his own special weapon — the *Laser Beam*. The 6½", battery-operated Commander-In-Chief of all *Zeroids* has power in this *Dyno Grid Arms* which energizes the *Laser Beam* making it light up and blink. *Zogg* himself lights up when switched on and he can move forward and backward. Battery operated. Uses 2 size AA batteries (not included.)"

Zeroid Alien Invader

The *Alien Zeroid*, as he has become known, was the most complex of the *Zeroid Robots*. He's not a true *Zeroid*, that is, he varies significantly from the design concept of the original *Zeroids*. "You control the alien, Insert the Action Program . . . watch him go", proclaims the box instructions. This "Invader from Outer Space with the Computer Brain" could be programmed with actions such as "Search", "Patrol", "Sentry", and "self-destruct" modes. The owner could program the *Alien* to drive in four different patterns by inserting "computer disks" into his back "cam cover." This robot, as with the original *Zeroid Robots*, could drive in forward and reverse with the switch of a toggle. The *Alien* had removable "body" pieces that included the head, both right and left "arms", and front computerized cover. The directional cams could be distinguished since they had holes located in each cam side. The hole designation indicated the programming of the cam. The cam with one hole indicated a self-destruct mode. The two-holed cam was a search cam. The three-holed cam was a patrol cam while the forth-holed cam was for sentry mode. The instructions gave specific instructions for the successful operation of the *Alien*. Under the section "How *Alien* Destructs", instructions indicated "After inserting cam, place *Alien* on floor and slide lever to forward. *Alien* will run straight ahead for a short distance then start to self destruct — first one arm then the other, then the head. Still up-right and running, *Alien* will make a half turn, fall over backwards and turn off.

★ 4776-1 ZEROIDS ASST.

Converting Cases

As I have discussed in the section Direct From The Planet Zero To You!, each *Zeroid* robot came with its own personal converting case, if you were fortunate enough as a child to receive the plexi-glass encased version of a *Mighty Zeroids Robot*.

Ideal Toys stated that *Zintar's* "case converts into a *Lunar Sled*." To enable the *Lunar Sled* to function, you were required to remove the clear plastic cover and turn the red colored *Lunar Sled* flat on its back. Flip the toggle switch and watch *Zintar* drive into his case. He could then speed off for some exploring of strange and alien lunar terrain, always with a watchful eye for the *Shag Monster* and its death defying grip.

Zerak "of the *Mighty Zeroids*" came complete in his very own "*Control Station*." "Turn him on while he's still in his control station package and lookout! His brute strength unhinges the transparent plastic cover which drops to provide an exit ramp for *Zerak*."

Zobor of the *Mighty Zeroids'* *Cosmobile* case also doubled as a play accessory. As with *Zintar's* *Lunar Sled*, the front clear cover needed to be removed. The yellow wheels could then be removed from the case and snapped into the legs. The *Cosmobile* could then be flipped over. Attach the *Cosmobile* onto the pin the extends from the back of *Zobor's* traction shield. *Zobor* and his *Cosmobile* are ready for any space action!

ZEM XXI Zeroid Explorer Module

The *Zem XXI* (21) *Zeroid Explorer Module* was a separate accessory item. This was a flying saucer-type spacecraft. It was brightly colored in a very 70's lime green and purple. The *Zeroid Explorer* didn't take batteries, but was rather operated by way of spring action. The three landing legs could be pulled out from the underside of the saucer and set to allow it to rest on any flat surface. The box description stated that the *Zeroid Explorer* had "automatic action." Flipping a lever on the belly of the flying saucer would allow the clear plastic canopy to begin to swing open, and, when it was in its final position, would drop the exit ramp down to the surface below. A pin located on the floor of the craft would activate a *Zeroid Robot* and the *Robot* (any *Robot* would fit) would drive down the ramp. And while all this was occurring, the spring action would make a "boink"ing sound. The box artwork stated that "platform rotates, landing pads automatically lower, ramp drops . . . *Zeroids* move out."

Solar Cycle

The *Solar Cycle* was a brightly colored lime green wheel. Any *Zeroid* but the *Alien* could power the solar cycle. Operation was simple. You placed a *Zeroid Robot* inside the *Solar Cycle* by fitting it underneath the plastic tabs and running guide. The "extra-terrestrial, circular treadmill converts the track power of the *Zeroid* into a rolling energy of its own. As the *Solar Cycle* rolls across alien planetscapes this galactic go-cart and *Zeroid* within it sways in curious pendulum motion."

Solar Cycle

Missile Defense Pad

Missile Defense Pad

The *Missile Defense Pad* was described in the Ideal Toys literature as "heavy weaponry designed to demonstrate the retaliatory capabilities of the peace-loving *Zeroids*. When the need arises, any *Zeroid*, moving up the pad ramp, will automatically trigger the sequential firing of three harmless spring-loaded rockets." Once the rockets were fired off, the *Zeroid* would automatically back down the ramp. This defense pad was designed in such a way that the trigger could be set and fired manually or to selectively fire from one to three rockets. The pad could be set at two different lengths and could be raised and lowered using the included four "stilts." The ramp section of the set could be set at any desired degree leading up to the rocket launch pad.

Sensor Station

The *Sensor Station*'s main mission was to act as the "eyes and ears of the *Zeroid* complex!" There are two types of *Sensor Station*. The first *Sensor Station* was included in

the *Command Set*, which included the *Commander Zogg Zeroid*. In this set, *Commander Zogg* would drive up to the *Sensor Station* platform with his *Dyno-Arms* extended in front of him. When *Zogg* comes into contact with the metal touch plates on the *Sensor Station*, he powers both the *Radar Dish* and *Power Antenna* which rotate a total of 360 degrees continuously. At the same time, the spinning *Hypno-Scope* informs *Commander Zogg* of new mission plans for further space exploration. The second type of *Sensor Station* was sold as a single accessory item. This *Station* did not require the energy supply from *Commander Zogg* to power it. Although looking the same as the first *Sensor Station*, this station required crank action to "rotate the antenna while a whirling symbol in the *Hypno-Scope* spins it's data to any *Zeroid* on Sentry duty." This futuristically designed, ever alert, precision-molded plastic structure with realistic control console details keeps the *Zeroid* installation safe and secure.

Sonic Alarm

The *Sonic Alarm* system was power by *Commander Zogg*. Operating in much the same way as the *Sensor Station*, *Zogg* extends his *Dyno-Arms* and comes into contact with the sensor pads on the *Alarm*. The *Sonic Alarm*, operating on *Zogg*'s unlimited power supply, screams out a sonic warning to all near by. Coded messages can be sent by hitting the round interrupt button on the base of the *Sonic Alarm*. "Whenever danger threatens and a warning signal must be given", *Commander Zogg* can fire up the *Sonic Alarm* station and send messages throughout the *Zeroid* complex.

Yellow Ramps

The Yellow Zeroid Ramps included in most packaging variations allowed a *Zeroid* to change direction when steered into the ramp. *Zintar, Zogg, Zemo, Zerak* or *Zobor* would roll forward under his own power onto the yellow ramp, immediately reversing direction awaiting his next mission assignment.

Sensor Station

STAR TEAM Toys 1969 – 1970 By Ideal Toys

Space Belt Set
This accessory pack, a large boxed item, included a child's-size utility belt, a gravity tool for picking up loose moon rocks and radioactive material, a plastic molded communicator, a brightly colored scope, and life support gear. All items were non-functional, plastic molded pieces.

Space Helmet
This real life *Space Helmet* was child-sized and molded in white plastic sporting a see through yellow tinted visor. Every explorer needed one of these to survive the rigors of deep space.

Space Boots
Every little boy and girl could prepare to go into space with Ideal Toys *Space Boots*. Slip these child-sized boots on and prepare for Star Trekking!

Remote Gripper
This was designed after the fashion of NASA's very own *Apollo* tools. Pick up space rocks, alien plants and red hot meteorites with this pincher-type tool. These orange and yellow plastic "Remote Grippers" made the *STAR TEAM* the ultimate space explorers.

STAR TEAM Toys 1977 – 1978 By Ideal Toys

The late-70's *Zeroid* robot lights up inside

Zeroid
This *Zeroid* was similar to the original *Zogg Zeroid*. For 1977, the *motorific* motor had been removed, rendering this *Zeroid* a push only toy. *Zeroid*, as he was now called, did still take a battery. It no longer powered "Dyno-grid" hands however. The *Zeroid* contained a torso light which, when switched on, blinked in rapid secession.

Zeroid And Star Hawk
The *Star Hawk* was a rehashed version of the *ZEM XXI Zeroid Explorer Module*. In fact, the same casting was utilized, so that it had the earlier copyright stamping in the base of the toy. How do you tell the difference? This *Star Hawk* was molded in red and black plastic, with a clear dome canopy. It still contained a dropping ramp and spring loaded rotating platform, as in the original *ZEM XXI*. Unlike the *ZEM XXI Module*, this *Star Hawk* ship did contain a *Zeroid*. It was the same design as the 1977 *Zeroid*, but with red inserts rather than blue inserts. It was not *motorific* powered.

Zem 21
Zem 21, in reality, was *Action Boy* in gold molded plastic from the hit toy series *Captain Action*. He was molded

---

Part 3 - Mighty Zeroid Robots and STAR TEAM

for this incarnation with circuitry on the outer skin of his arms, legs and chest. He was given an alien looking green head and was fully jointed and articulated.

Knight Of Darkness

This black caped and uniformed figure looked foreboding. With his bowling ball-like head, and fully jointed and articulated body, he was ready for any space war. This figure, formally known as *Captain Action*, worked well as the evil *Knight of Darkness*. With a little remolding, *Captain Action* had been transformed. Little was changed from the *Captain Action* figure now molded in black. The lighting bolts on the boots were still present, as was his *Space Lazer* pistol. This had been lifted from *Captain Action*'s Flash Gordon, but made a successful transition to this space warring figure.

Kent And Cosmic Cruiser

Kent was a 9" action figure wearing a brightly colored red suit with silver accents. The suit was reminiscent of *Mork* space suit from the hit show *Mork And Mindy*. This figure, as with both the *Knight of Darkness* and *Zem 21*, was manufactured using hard plastic. The figure was poseable at arm, elbow, leg and knee joints. *Kent* was packaged with his *Cosmic Cruiser*. This was a "space hero every kid could identify with ... and the star cruiser that could take him on missions to the far reaches of the galaxy!" The *Cosmic Cruiser* boasted a computer control panel and authentic *STAR TEAM* insignia and markings. It had wheels located on the underside and like the *Zeroid*, was a push toy.

19 TOYS

ZEM 21® TV
4602-9
Zem 21 stands 9" tall, he's fully poseable, and his jointed humanoid body is designed with all the mechanical chrome styling of a real super-science robot of tomorrow. He's not a leader, though—he needs a Zeroid companion to do his thinking for him.
But what an action pair Zem 21 and Zeroid make together!
Pack: 12 pcs. Wgt: 11 lbs.

KNIGHT OF DARKNESS® TV
4603-7
Ideal's Knight of Darkness: somber, powerful, an 11½" fully poseable figure in imperial black cape, black and silver uniform, with a grim masked head that strikes terror into the bravest heart!
In his hand, a futuristic weapon. Black boots, black hands complete his menacing appearance. The Knight of Darkness—perfect bad guy for long hours of imagination and excitement.
Pack: 12 pcs. Wgt: 14 lbs.

ZEROID® TV
4600-3
Zeroids are sold separately, too—a perfect way for kids to add to their Star Team strength.
Individual Zeroids have blue accents and stripes.
With more than one Zeroid to share the brain-work, the Star Team has an even better chance against the Knight of Darkness! (2 AA batteries not included.)
Pack: 12 pcs. Wgt: 11 lbs.

Part 3 - Mighty Zeroid Robots and STAR TEAM

The Creation Of A Roid

Major Matt Mason was the first astronaut figure released for Mattel's *Man in Space* toy line in 1967, with a flurry of toys and accessories following. The rush was on, and toy companies from the mid-1960's were all vying for the consumer dollar, wanting to meet the needs of parents wishing to fulfill their own fantasies and their children's dreams. So, where did the *Zeroids* come from? The Ideal Toy Company had a lot of robot experience under their belt by the time *Zeroids* were created. These robots were a wonderful companion for Mattel's team of astronauts, and themes of these two rival toy company products were similar. If you've been fortunate enough to see *Zeroid Robots* up close, a few questions my come to mind. Did

you ever wonder why *Zerak* looks so different from his *Zeroid* brothers, *Zintar* and *Zobor*? The most significant reason was that *Zerak* was not designed exclusively in and for the United States. *Zerak* was designed in the UK, and shows a very different styling theme. First, his body is radically different from the others, and few parts were shared. He has a much more traditional leg design. *Zerak* has three eyes. *Zerak* is not a kind and peaceful *Zeroid*, or inquisitive explorer, but rather he is described as a "destroyer." *Zerak*'s case continues the contrast between he and the other *Zeroids*. His case is not a plexi-glass lid, but is a hinged and fold down unit. Even the casing was provided with a difference in theme. Whereas *Zintar* and *Zobor* cases were designed for exploratory missions and transport, *Zerak*'s case was meant to be used as part of a command base. In fact, Ideal's literature refers to the case as a "control station."

The *Zerak* robot was designed in the UK

Zintar, who seems to be the most popular of all the *Zeroids*, was described as the "explorer." *Zintar* and *Zobor* share many design features. The theme of space exploration is a commonality. Both have similar style bodies, without legs and antennae. *Zintar* shares similar design traits with another wildly popular robot of the mid 1960's — *Robot* from *Lost In Space*, produced by Remco. *Zobor* also shares design traits with yet another popular 1960's robot — *Rosie* from the *Jetsons* cartoon show is very similar to the final design that became *Zobor*. *Zogg* didn't look like any of the *Zeroids* that came before him. He was a slightly later product, and was designed with very different traits from *Zintar*, *Zobor*

Robot from the TV series *Lost In Space*

and *Zerak*. He was thought to be the teacher of the *Zeroids*, their commander-in-chief. Note the chrome flat antennae on the top of *Zogg*'s "head." Does this appear to be a graduation cap? Of course, as you already know, *Zogg* came with his *Commander Set*, and, with his *Dyno-Grid* hands, could operate all accessory items. As the 1970's approached, children's interest in space and science fiction toys appeared to be waning. The United States had successfully landed the first man on the moon and space travel appeared to be becoming commonplace. Both Ideal *Zeroids* and Mattel's *Major Matt Mason* toys took on a new flavor in styling. The toys moved further away from realism, and box artwork became much more colorful and dynamic. The *Talking Flying Major Matt Mason* box, with its bright hues of purple and lime green, paralleled what was happening at Ideal with the *Zeroids*. Enter the *Alien Invader*. This *Zeroid*, and I use that term very loosely, didn't really have anything to do with *Zeroids*. It didn't look like a *Zeroid*, and it didn't have the mechanical action of a *Zeroid*. It utilized a cog system to direct its movements, and could even self-destruct. The box for the *Alien* was wild, especially compared with the darker illustrated boxes of the early *Zeroids*. You couldn't get much brighter than the purple and pink that was used for that box. Bright lime green and yellow writing stated boldly that here was a dynamic NEW *Zeroid*. that you must see! *Zemo*, is a *Zeroid* who you've probably never heard of (I've been collecting *Zeroids* for ten years and was

Zemo, although very rare, is a genuine Zeroid

not, in fact, aware of his existence until about two years ago, and then, amazingly, I was able to purchase one for myself.) Zemo is far and away the most rare of any *Zeroid* known to date. *Zemo* was produced by Ideal. It's not a rip-off toy, nor has it been assembled and passed off as an original. *Zemo* does exist. This robot came at the end of *Zeroid* production and was sold through five and dime stores. My *Zemo*, which is red in color, was sold for a mere 68 cents through Kresges department stores. The stock number identifies it as 4777-9. *Zemo* was really an inexpensive way to make another *Zeroid* product. As much as he was an original design, he had many similarities with the Chrysler Corporation's K Car series. Virtually all of *Zemo*'s parts were taken from the first three *Zeroid Robots*. *Zemo* had the track and "legs" of *Zobor* with his torso and arms sourced from *Zerak*. *Zemo*'s head was from *Zintar*. It's interesting to note that, although at first glance, *Zemo* appears to have taken these parts from the other *Zeroids* with no

variations, this is not, in fact, the case. On closer examination, *Zemo*'s detailing it unique. An example is the grill on his base. This design appears to have been copied from *Zobor* however, even though *Zobor*'s grill is a solid molded piece, whereas *Zemo*'s grill is a separate, black molded accessory. The four small grills on the top of the base are, again, molded as part of the body on *Zobor*, yet separate inset pieces on *Zemo*. The flat square chromed piece that joins *Zemo*'s "legs" to his lower body are unique to this robot and not shared with the others. Finally, the small buttons that are located on *Zintar*'s "legs" were relocated and sit on the top of *Zemo*'s base. I've included close ups of *Zemo* showing both the similarities and the differences with the other *Zeroids* for comparison purposes. If you every come across *Zemo*, in either red or aqua color, I would suggest purchasing him — he's an extremely rare *Zeroid Robot* indeed.

Ideal Toys And The Advertising Formula For Success!

The Ideal Toy Company, like Mattel and Colorform, although to a lesser extent, saw a dramatic decline in sales of their once *Mighty Zeroid Robots* as the world left the 1960's behind and entered a new decade. Ideal had always utilized the media and television medium to their advantage with *Zeroids*, and to great success. Department store wishbooks of the late 1960's attest

STAR TEAM mini comic book

to that fact. Many pages of pictures and text can be found of *Zeroids*. The *STAR TEAM* was no exception. Simpson-Sears, Canada's Eaton stores, J.C Penny and Kresges all had their fair share of *Zeroid Robots*. And *STAR TEAM* toys were the same. Sears catalogues were always a favorite, especially their Christmas wishbooks. In 1970, on page 47, they showed the introduction of the *STAR TEAM* toys by Ideal with the slogan "Its great to pretend you're walking on the moon." For a mere $9.88 you could purchase both the *Space Helmet* and *Space Boots*. For just $5.99 Sears was more than happy to sell the *Equipment belt*, along with the *Space Dog*, *Space Saucer* and *Space Robot* magic dial toys. The *Naughty Robot* "walks and twists like a dancer" was the *STAR TEAM* advertisement. It stated "Space Helmet and Boots. Space helmet of amber gold-colour break-resistant plastic fits all sizes. Collar has finned louvers and vent for receiving life support Headphone non-operative. Molded plastic air-cushioned boots have laces, adjust to fit. Large lugged soles leave impressive footprints, and low pitched whistle accents each step. For ages 5 to 10 years."

Ideal, going to additional expense in the year 1977 to promote the *STAR TEAM*, released a mini comic book. This comic showed great action artwork on the cover. *CP30*, I mean *Zem 21*, *Zeroid* and the *Star Hawk*

were all illustrated, as was the evil *Knight of Darkness*. "Join *Zem 21* and the *Zeroids*, as they battle the *Knight of Darkness* and his *Raiders of the Black Nebula!* Ideal exclaimed "Journey to the Future! It is the year 3000. For the first time, Earth's solar system faces invasion! From out of the mysterious *Black Nebular*, which swirls in the interstellar vastness beyond Pluto, have come the *Knight of Darkness* and his *Shadow Warriors* to establish a foothold amid the outer planets of the Solar System. Here, they have been held at bay but the *Knight*'s drive for conquest is unending. To keep him in check required constant vigilance. And this dangerous vigil is the job of Earth's *STAR TEAM* Scouts, such as *Zem 21* and his two *Zeroid* companions, the heroic crew of the saucer ship *Star Hawk*." Ideal Toys and Marvel comic's . . . *STAR TEAM* comics were produced by Marvel Comics Group in conjunction with Ideal Toy Corp.

The story unfolds in a galaxy far, far away . . . "The *Star Hawk* is on patrol near the ringed plane of Saturn. For now, it is quiet, but *STAR TEAM* scouts can never be certain when they will suddenly have to face *Raiders of the Black Nebular*! Reverse course *Zeroid Red*! I believe I saw something on that moon we just passed! Yes there, it is wrecked cruisers of the *Shadow Warriors* . . . take us down *Zeroid Red*. That is not our mission . . . correct *Zeroid blue*? Affirmative . . . we are hunting active enemy ships, not wrecks, *Zem 21*. You *Zeroids* always stick together. But you're programmed as an engineer / mechanic, *Blue* . . . And your duty is as pilot / gunner, *Red*. But . . . along with recording and analyzing data, I make plans for the team . . . and right how, the plan is to enrich my data banks with information about that wreck! Soon, *Zem 21*, your need for data always leads to trouble! it is as bad as human curiosity. Correction *Zeroid Red*, it is worse! Suddenly . . . *Blue*! You're blinking like a beacon light, What . . . Danger Danger . . . my sensors detect . . . machinery operation . . . there is activity within that ship. *Shadow Warriors* of the *Knight of Darkness*? Retreat to the *Star Hawk, Blue*." The comic continues with a battle ensuing . . . The *Knight of Darkness*

appears shooting *Zem 21* . . . "No one escapes me, Robot . . . be grateful . . . my blaster merely paralyzes your motor circuits . . ." The *Knight* continues on explaining how his warriors will take over Earth as they are now within striking distance of the Space Fleet! *Zem 21*, seeing his shipmate *Zeroids* shoot down attacks the *Knight* turning off the control panel disabling the wrecked ship. The *Knight of Darkness* commands his *Warriors* to "get him . . . catch that clanking clown. Dodging blaster fire . . . *Zem 21* tries to flee the chamber but all the exits have been sealed. *Zem 21* is cornered by the *Knight* . . . just like your fate robot; my uniblaster is now set to melt you into a puddle of molten metal! But suddenly . . . near the control panel . . . a warrior yells . . . look it is some kind of drill. It is connected to those infernal *Zeroids*! An explosion occurs and the *Zeriods* make for *Zem 21*. Join us while I keep them busy with my shock blasts instructs *Zeroid Red*. The *Zeroids* then, working as a team, cross the matter transmitters and cause an overload. Curse *Zem 21* add those two *Zeroids* exclaims the *Knight of Darkness* . . . Still, the three robots are able to reach their saucer craft and blast off . . . Just in time! *Red and Blue*, I believe the *Knight of Darkness* has been taught a valuable lesson when it comes to faking a space ship crash. Affirmative *Zem 21* and whatever his next plans are . . . the *STAR TEAM* scouts will be better at THAT too!"

STAR TEAM pin-up included with the mini comic book

Here they come...from the Planet Zero!
The incredible workers of the Future!

ZEROIDS™

Moving across the landscape, overrunning all obstacles as inexorably as the Future itself, these amazing, efficient and powerful automatons have but one purpose — to serve their masters (your customers) at work and play!

Each Zeroid has a unique pair of special purpose hands, interchangeable magnetic and throwing hands, and a battery-powered motor with forward and reverse drive. In operation, Zeroids are capable of grabbing, pinching, carrying, clawing, attracting, throwing, pushing, pulling or hauling functions.

From "turret to track" each Zeroid simulates a marvelous mechano-electronic complex, molded in awesome detail, and the sparkling Zeroid packages double as functional play units!

4773-B ZINTAR

4772-0 ZOBOR

4771-2 ZERAK

As seen on TV

Part 3 - Mighty Zeroid Robots and STAR TEAM

Zeroids operate on 2 AA type batteries (Batteries not included)

4771-2 ZERAK—THE BLUE DESTROYER—"Turn him on" while he's still in his control station package and lookout! His brute strength unhinges the transparent plastic cover which drops to provide an exit ramp for Zerak. Employs unique hooks for hands plus magnetic and throwing hands.

4772-0 ZOBOR—THE BRONZE TRANSPORTER—A kindly carrier with special duty gripper claws. Like magic, his empty plastic package becomes a roomy Cosmobile for hauling loads. Also has magnetic and throwing hands.

4773-8 ZINTAR—THE SILVER EXPLORER—The back portion of this Zeroid's package becomes a dramatic lunar sled that seems to carry gripper-fisted Zintar over the terrain. With magnetic and throwing hands.

Each of the above—Pack per doz.: 6/12   Wgt.: 8½ lbs.

4776-1 ZEROID ASST. DEAL—Contains 1 doz. 3 styles asstd.
Pack: 1 deal per carton   Weight: 17 lbs.

- Look! Zeroid pack doubles as play accessory!
- Each Zeroid equipped with magnetic hands, throwing hands, lazer bomb & reversing ramp!

Part 3 - Mighty Zeroid Robots and STAR TEAM

Product Catalogues

The 1968 through 1970 Ideal Toys product catalogues included colorful photography of most bubble cards and boxed toys. Ideal Toys went to the expense of including full-page dioramas of their *Mighty Zeroid Robots* in action showing the *Zogg Command Set* in full working order. The photographs below depict all *Zeriods* fully interacting with their *Zeroid* accessories. *Zogg* is powering his red *Sonic Station*. The *Sensor Station* can be seen in full color. *Zerak* demonstrates how to travel in the *Solar Cycle*, while *Zintar* prepares to fire the yellow, blue and red rockets from the *Zeroid Missile Defense* pad. *Zerak*, *Zobor* and *Zintar* are pictured in action demonstrating their mini playset case action. One can almost see *Zintar* powered by his *motorific* motor, racing across the kitchen floor, with the slight acidic smell and high pitched whine of his high revving engine as he makes one more pass in wild cat territory! Photos of the *Alien Invader Zeroid* and his impossible-to-find cogs appear together. Note the similar casting of the *STAR TEAM Star Hawk* and the much earlier *ZEM XXI*. Decals are changed but the molding and spring action remains the same.

"As seen on TV"

"Here they come…from the Planet Zero! The incredible workers of the Future!"
Zeroids
proudly proclaimed Ideal Toys.

Their catalogue set the stage for the *Mighty Zeriods* . . ."Moving across the landscape, overrunning all obstacles as inexorable as the Future itself, these amazing, efficient and powerful automatons have but one purpose — to serve their masters (your customers) at work and play!"

Each *Zeroid* has a unique pair of special purpose hands, interchangeable magnetic and throwing hands, and battery-powered motor with forward and reverse drive. In operation, *Zeroids* are capable of grabbing, pinching, carrying, clawing, attracting throwing, pushing, pulling or hauling functions.

From "turret to track" each *Zeroid* simulates a marvelous machine-electronic complex, molded in awesome detail, and the sparkling *Zeroid* packages double as functional play units!

4771-2 *Zerak – The Blue Destroyer* — Turn him on while he's still in his *Control Station* package and lookout! His brute strength unhinges the transparent plastic cover, which drops to provide an exit ramp for *Zerak*. Employs unique hooks for hands plus magnetic and throwing hands.

4772-0 *Zobor – The Bronze Transporter* — A kindly carrier with special duty gripper claws. Like magic, his empty plastic package becomes a roomy *Cosmobile* for hauling loads. Also has magnetic and throwing hands.

4773-8 *Zintar – The Silver Explorer* — The back portion of this *Zeroid*'s package becomes a dramatic *Lunar Sled* that seems to carry gripper-fisted *Zintar* over the terrain. With magnet and throwing hands.

"Each of our swingin Zeroids is still doing its own special "thing". Every kid feels he has to have them all! In their new shelf-talking, stack-packing packages, *Zeroids* present a sparkling and self-selling, irresistible display."

4659-9 *Alien Invader* — He may look somewhat mean and menacing, but he's really a mass of mirth provoking mechanicals. Using four cams included the *Alien Invader* will search a zigzag course, walk past Sentry-fashion, Patrol the area in a square pattern . . . or . . . Self-destruct. First, his right arm falls off, then his left arm . . . then his head blows off . . . and now *Alien Invader* falls on his back as his motor turns off!

4764-7 *Zeroid With Solar Cycle* — An extra-terrestrial, circular treadmill, 9" in diameter, that converts the track power of the included *Zeroid* into a rolling energy of its own.

4649-0 *Defense Pad* — Heavy weaponry designed to demonstrate the capabilities of the peace-loving *Zeroids*. The missiles may be launched manually and selectively.

4648-2 – *Sensor Station* — The eyes and ears of for the *Zeroids*. No *Zeroid* installation can be considered safe without this ever-alert warning system.

4606-8-6 – *Zem XXI* — This is exactly what happens when the switch is thrown on the amazing *Zeroid Exploratory Module*: First, an eerie beeping sound is heard . . . alerting all of the arrival of an outer-space visitor. Then, slowly the ship's transparent plastic canopy turns . . . while it lowers its landing pads, establishing itself on terra firma. When the canopy reaches the open position — an unloading ramp lowers into position — and any *Zeroid* happening to be inside *ZEM XXI* is automatically triggered to exit down the ramp. It's an eye-popping, out-of-this-world sight for sure! *ZEM XXI* is 13" in diameter and 9" high. The interior is appointed with realistic-looking flight control console. The *Zeroid Exploratory Module* is mechanically operated — no batteries required. Closing the plastic canopy cocks the operating mechanism in preparation for the next exploratory trip.

4763-9 – *Zogg With Laser Beam* — *Zogg*, the number one motorized *Zeroid* of them all is now available with his own special weapon — the *Laser Beam*! The 6½" battery-operated *Zeroid* has power in his Arms which energizes the *Laser Beam*. *Zogg* himself lights up and can move backwards and forwards.

STAR TEAM wins the Space Race!

"STAR TEAM, from Ideal — fantastic action figures that bring the future down to earth today. Stalwart heroes, menacing villains, lovable robots and space vehicles that conquer the space system."

"Join the STAR TEAM ... let Ideal help you capture all the sellout demand created by the science fiction boom!"

4601-1 – *Zeroid And Star Hawk* — The original STAR TEAM robot and starship! *Zeroid* is a friendly, intelligent 5½" tall robot with red accent stripes, moveable arms, rubber treads and a blinking light in his head that shows his brain is working full time. He's lovable, but he's got the key strategies the STAR TEAM needs to defeat the *Knight of Darkness*. His *Star Hawk* is 14" in diameter, a super interplanetary vehicle with transparent cockpit dome, computer instrument panel, three pods for landing, a mechanical airlock door that makes a weird outer-space sound when it opens, even a retractable ramp for *Zeroid* to disembark. Open the door, and legs and ramp extend automatically. *Zeroid* and *Star Hawk* .. . super member of Ideal's STAR TEAM!

4602-9 – ZEM 21 — *Zem 21* stands 9" tall, he's fully poseable and his jointed humanoid body is designed with all the mechanical chrome styling of a real super-science robot of tomorrow. He's not a leader, though — he needs a *Zeroid* companion to do his thinking for him. But what an action pair *Zem 21* and *Zeroid* make together.

4603-7 – Ideal's *Knight of Darkness* — Somber, powerful, an 11½" fully poseable figure in imperial black cape, black and silver uniform, with grim masked head that strikes terror into the bravest heart! In his hand, a futuristic weapon. Black boots, black hands complete his menacing appearance. The *Knight of Darkness* — perfect bad guy for long hours of imagination and excitement.

4600-3 – *Zeroids* are sold separately, too — Perfect way for kids to add to their STAR TEAM strength. Individual *Zeroids* have blue accents and stripes. With more than one *Zeroid* to share the brainwork, the STAR TEAM has an even better chance against the *Knight of Darkness*!

4606-0 – *Kent and his Cosmic Cruiser* — Here's the space hero every kid can identify with ... and the star cruiser that can take him on missions to the far reaches of the galaxy! *Kent* stands 9" tall, blasts through space in his *Cosmic Cruiser* or leaves his vehicle for adventures on distant planets. He's fully poseable, with STAR TEAM coverall uniform and helmet. The *Cosmic Cruiser* looks like a real space vehicle: blunt nose for re-entry, computer control panel, authentic STAR TEAM insignia and markings, with wheels for push play action on any surface. *Kent and his Cosmic Cruiser* ... Ideal's STAR TEAM leader in the space race of 1978.

Direct From The Planet Zero To You

Zeroids And STAR TEAM Toys

As noted earlier, *Zeroid Robots* were an extension of our real life drama. Preparation for our first mission to the stars was in the works. Science fiction television interest was at an all time high, the Viet Nam war raged on, and the public searched for a diversion from the chaos in the streets and campuses across our great country. Ideal Toys stepped up to the challenge, creating the *Zeroid Robots* from the planet Zero.

The following chapter itemizes each toy in the *Zeroid* and STAR TEAM toy line. Each toy is identified by stock number and official name. Details of the figure or accessory are provided along with breakdown of items included in the box or on blister card. I have, as often as possible, included a picture of the exterior of the box or blister card (for easy reference) as well as the contents of both the cards and boxed sets.

Zeroids From The *Planet Zero* — 1967-1971 Product Line

Stock Number: 4773-8
Item Name: ***Zintar of the Mighty Zeroids***
Copyright Date: 1968
Contents:
This gray robot with *motorific* power plant was sold with his red plastic mini playset case.
Accessories:
Zintar was sold with his yellow reversing ramp. *Zintar* came with spring loaded thumbed claws. Additional accessory items included his *bomb*, *funnel* and *magnet* hand.
Packaging:
Elaborate plexi-glass packaging with outer beautifully detailed header card.

Stock Number: 4772-0
Item Name: ***Zobor of the Mighty Zeroids***
Copyright Date: 1968
Contents:
Copper colored plastic robot. Two AA-size batteries powered this *Zeroid*.
Accessories:
Zobor was sold with his hands, two adjustable claws, plus accessory *bomb* and *funnel* with *magnet* hand. This robot included a yellow reversing ramp in his plastic clear plexi-glass casing.
Packaging:
Zobor was sold in a teal-colored *Cosmobile* case that had large yellow wheels which could be attached to allow the *Cosmobile* to become a sort of galactic

Part 3 - *Mighty Zeroid Robots* and *Star Team*

pickup truck. A tall header card with elaborate and detailed instructions "sold" this toy to both kids and parents alike.

Stock Number: 4771-2
Item Name: ***Zerak of the Mighty Zeroids***
Copyright Date: 1968
Contents:

Zerak was sold in a gray plastic case, which doubled as a play set. *Zerak* operated on two AA-size batteries powering his *motorific* engine, which fit into the base of this robot. His hands, again different than the other *Zeroids*, were red plastic hook like claws.

Accessories:

Zerak was sold with a yellow reversing ramp, but, unlike *Zobor* and *Zintar*, his did not sit at the front of the case. He was also sold with accessory hands. *Funnel* and *bomb* were standard *Zeroid* issue.

Packaging:

This mini case doubled as a *Control Station* with a clear lowering ramp — actually the clear cover that was hinged to drop onto the ground. The header card for this robot continues a similar theme with alien planetscape and mountainous cliffs in the foreground.

Stock Number: 4773-8
Item Name: ***Zintar of the Mighty Zeroids***
Copyright Date: 1968
Contents:

Contents and Accessories were identical to the header carded *Zeroid* toys *Zerak* and *Zobor*.

Packaging:

The package for this *Zeroid* toy, rather than utilizing the above header-card, made use of a elaborately printed carded sleeve that fit over the exterior of the red plastic backing and clear plastic cover.

Part 3 - *Mighty Zeroid Robots* and *STAR TEAM*

Stock Number: 4772-0
Item Name: *Zobor of the Mighty Zeroids*
Copyright Date: 1968
Contents:
    Contents and accessories were again the same as the header-carded *Zeroid* toy.

Packaging:
    Zobor's bright green and mustard yellow sleeve box made for a flashy display. The lower left tab at the bottom of the box front identified in bright red coloring that this robot toy was "motorized."

Stock Number: 4771-8
Item Name: *Zerak of the Mighty Zeroids*
Copyright Date: 1968
Contents:
    Contents and accessories were again the *bomb, funnel* hand and reversing ramp.
Packaging:
    This was the nicest of the "sleeve" boxed *Zeroid* toys. This sleeve box looked so much better, I believe,

because the plexi-case wasn't flat, but bowed out and displayed better the insides of the box. The box itself was a bright yellow at the top, changing colors midway to a reddish-orange color. The front base of the card sleeve stated "case converts into *Control Station*."

Stock Number: 4763-9
Item Name: *Zogg of the Mighty Zeroids*
Copyright Date: 1968
Contents:
    This boxed "sleeve" set was produced, albeit possibly in extremely limited quantities. I know that past *Zeroid* publications and articles have frequently stated that *Zogg* was only sold in his *Command Set*, but this isn't accurate, based on new photos and information.
Packaging:
    The 1970 Ideal Toys catalogue does show a boxed *Zogg* similar in design to the other three *Zeroid* Robots. The catalogue has assigned a product number and states that *Zogg* is sold with his *Laser Beam*. The box art looks intriguing. The overall sleeve color is mauve, and *Zogg* sits inside a yellow plastic molded casing background. The top of this card shows *Zogg* written in large block letters, illustrated in light blue, and highlighted in white print. Beneath the name is

the now-familiar *Zeroids* printed in a black background. As with the other *Zeroids*, the "Z" is printed in bright a red color with "eroids" printed in white.

Stock Number: 4662-3
Item Name: *Zintar*
Copyright Date: 1968
Contents:
   Zintar continued to be packaged with his spring loaded and "jointed" thumbs, and driven by his *motorific* motor.
Accessories:
   The yellow reversing ramp was deleted from the list of accessory items. *Zintar* did continue to be packaged with either a yellow or black *bomb*, his *funnel* and *magnet* hand.
Packaging:
   Generic bubble cards now replaced the previous *Zeroid Robot*-specific header cards and / or "sleeved" cards. The *Robots* were now identified on their cards

only as *Zeroids*. *Zintar* did still have his name embossed in silver on his torso. The tag line "of the *Mighty Zeroids*" was now nowhere to be found on the box artwork.

Stock Number: 4597-1
Item Name: *Zobor*
Copyright Date: 1968
Contents:
   Zobor, in this incarnation of packaging and cost saving, continues on with his engine and his lobster-like claw hands.
Accessories:
   The *bomb*, the *funnel* and the *magnet* have remained, but the ramp, as with *Zintar*, has been deleted.
Packaging:
   Generic bubble cards with the individuality and personality of the robots taken away — now referred to only generically as *Zeroids*.

Stock Number: 4596-3
Item Name: *Zerak*
Copyright Date: 1968
Contents:
   Zerak has lost his *Control Station*. He has also lost his yellow reversing ramp, but has kept his motor and his claw-like hook hands.
Accessories:
   As with all *Zeroids* on bubble cards, *Zerak* gets his obligatory additional hands.
Packaging:
   With no case to come busting out of, and no ramp to

glide down, *Zerak* looks less menacing and less interesting. Cost saving begins to take its toll on the once *Mighty Zeroids*.

Stock Number: 4777-9
Item Name: **Robot**
Copyright Date: 1968
Contents:

Zintar, Zerak, Zobor, Zogg, and the newest addition to the family, *Zemo,* were now identified only by their names being embossed on their torsos. They continued to be manufactured with their motor and with generic "*Robot*" instruction sheets, which were all now identical. Ideal Toys continued to place the correct "hands" on each of the *Robots. Zemo* is interesting in that not all the *Zemo's* made actually had their name embossed on their torsos like the others. The aqua colored *Zemo* that I have seen does, in fact, say *Zemo.* To complicate matters, however, the red *Zemo* in my current collection of *Zeroids,* the only one I have ever seen, doesn't have his *Zemo* name embossed on his torso. He is identified as only "*Robot*" on both the instruction sheet and the box artwork. Incidentally, *Zemo* has the hands of *Zerak.*

Accessories:

Included with all *Robots* were the additional "hands" — *funnel, magnet* and *bomb. Zogg* was an exception. *Zogg,* still powered by two AA-size batteries, remained somewhat superior to the others, and was sold with his *Laser Beam* attachment.

Generic packaging used by Kresges

Packaging:

You couldn't get much more basic than the packaging from Kresges stores. Was this box ever cheap and basic! Blue line illustrations identified that inside the box was a *Robot.* To identify which robot was included, you needed to peer into a small window in the box. The window did not originally have cello on it. A basic cardboard track base and neck brace held the robot in place. Placement of the robot inside the box was so bad as to make it almost impossible to see which robot you were looking at through the

window. The top and the bottom of the box were glued as well as taped to ensure that accessories didn't fall out. They sat in a shelf-like area just under the box lid. A final note on these *Zeroids* was they, in fact, were considered generic, so much so that they actually only had one stock number for all six robot designs.

Stock Number: T3135
Item Name: **Zerak Robot / Zintar**
Copyright Date: 1968
Contents:

The OK Toy Company didn't include accessories with their version of the *Zerak* Robots. In this incarnation, they were no longer called *Zeroids,* and the *Zeroid* tag line wasn't used. They were still identified, as with Kresges version, with embossed names on their chests.

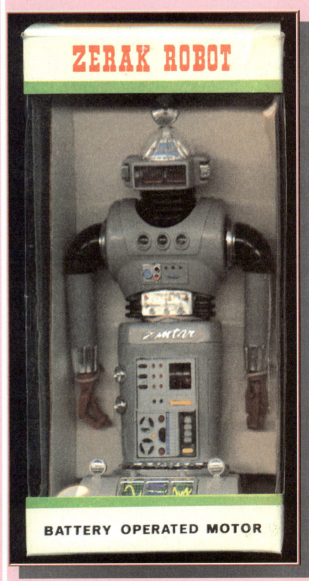

The OK Company *Zintar* labeled as "Zerak"

Accessories:

There were no longer additional "hands" included with any of the *Zerak* robots. No *funnel* hands, *bombs* or *magnet* hands, and long ago the yellow reversing ramps had been discontinued. The "battery operated robots" did continue to include the *motorific* engine that was placed inside the robot for shipping.

Packaging:

A much smaller and less elaborate box with a cello window was now used to sell these *Zerak* robots. A white card insert and pink twist ties held the robot in place. Instructions to operate the robot were now printed on the bottom of the card box.

Stock Number: T3134
Item Name: ***Zerak Robot / Zobor***
Copyright Date: 1968
Contents:

The Robot.

Accessories:

Motorific power plant.

Packaging:

All the *Zerak* robots made do with the same box. Incidentally, there is no *Zemo* robot displayed on the photo box artwork.

Stock Number: T3133
Item Name: ***Zerak Robot / Zerak***
Copyright Date: 1968
Contents:

The Robot.

Accessories:

Motorific power plant.

Packaging:

This is truly the only box that looks correct for the OK Company robots. The name of course fits the robot included in this box, given that this robot is really *Zerak*. It's anyone's guess as to why the OK Company chose the name *Zerak* and put it on all boxes, regardless of the robot contained within.

Stock Number: T3425
Item Name: ***Zerak Robot / Zogg***
Copyright Date: 1968
Contents:

The Robot.

Accessories:

The power plant continued to be offered for *Zogg*. It should be noted, however, that his *Laser Beam* was not an included accessory. He did continue to direct power through his dyno hands. He continued with the mechanism that permitted this robot to use his torso as a light beacon.

Packaging:

The generic theme of the boxes continues with *Zogg*, since there was no differentiation between this robot

The OK Company *Zerak*

and the other boxes.

Note:

The *Zemo Zeroid* robot was not packaged, nor was he available in the OK company packaging.

Stock Number: 4608-6
Item Name: ***ZEM XXI Zeroid Explorer Module***
Copyright Date: 1970
Contents:

Zem XXI was a self-contained flying saucer-type ship. Many collectors assume that it came with a *Zeroid Robot*, it didn't. This was an accessory item that had to be purchased separately, as indicated on the exterior the *Zem XXI* box. *Zem* didn't have any separate parts, coming complete inside a plastic wrap. Attached to the ship was the clear dome and three landing pod legs. The only items separate from the ship were the small decal sheet and double-sided instructions.

Accessories:

No accessories were included with this item.

Packaging:

Zem XXI came in a very large square box. The saucer was held in place by two white cardboard inserts. The top insert allowed the dome of the *ZEM XXI* to slip through a round hole supporting the ship from moving inside the box. The larger bottom insert supported the base and three landing legs of the craft. The applied outer box graphic was very colorful and adhered to the "front" of the box only. The sides and top of the box were illustrated with purple writing and line illustrations.

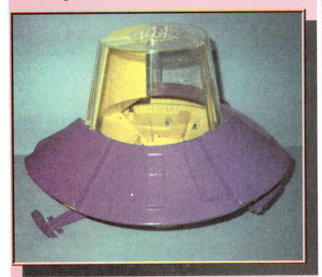

The ZEM XXI Explorer Module

Stock Number: 4659-9
Item Name: *Alien Invader*
Copyright Date: 1970

Contents:

The *Alien*, as he has become known, came packaged inside a very large fully illustrated and colored box. The *Alien* was able to complete many self-destruct and "remote control" functions. This robot came complete with molded stump-like "arms", thick tree-like trunk, and domed head. He appeared to have been molded to look like he was melting. This was a good thing since this robot suffered from the same chemical reaction problem as *Major Matt Mason* and some of his accessories. If you're fortunate enough to find an *Alien*, he'll probably have melt marks on his upper torso and arms where a chemical reaction between the two plastics has occurred over time.

Accessories:

This robot didn't have accessories, per say. However, to program it to self-destruct, as well as complete other "remote control" actions, four cogs were included in the packaging. A detailed instruction sheet

was also included.

Packaging:

The *Alien Invader* came in a large box, similar in size to the old *Ker-plunk* game. Inside the box was a bubbled header-type card. The *Alien* was attached similar to the bubbled *Zeroids*, with his four cogs contained under the bubble itself. It's almost impossible to find the *Alien* complete and functioning with both box and card complete and in mint condition. This was a highly inventive toy, but in many ways, other than having the *Zeroid* name on its box, had little to do with the original *Zeroid Robots*.

Stock Number: 4764-7
Item Name: *Zeroid with Solar Cycle*
Copyright Date: 1970

Contents:

The *Zeroid and Solar Cycle* was a generic boxed item. Packaged in this colorful mauve and blue lunarscaped box was the lime green *Solar Cycle*, the same *Cycle* that was included with both the *Zeroid Commander Action Set* and the *Zeroid Action Set*. The *Zeroid and Solar Cycle* boxed set included any one of the three original robots, *Zintar*, *Zerak* or *Zobor*. The stock number was the same for all three robot types, regardless of which *Zeroid* was included.

Accessories:

This boxed set is very rare and beautifully put together. Accessories included the aforementioned *hands*, *magnet* and *bomb*, and of course the reversing ramp.

Packaging:

The box for this toy is really what makes the item. Standing just over 12" in height, the front of the box was designed as a perforated window which could be lowered to display the *Zeroid* robot inside. The top of the window was a flip up design which fit underneath the lid top. The boxing of this variation of the *Mighty Zeroids* included colored illustration of all *Zeroids* on both the face of the box (racing across the lunarscape) and on each side of the box. *Zeroids* were depicted in action mode. The rear of the box provided highly detailed instructions on such topics as "motor installation, battery installation, how to operate the arms, switch operation, automatic reversing ramp, removal and replacement of hands, and installation of *Zeroid* in *Solar Cycle*." Note: This item is unique to the *Zeroid* line of toys due to a specific notation on the front of the box: "MCMLXIX Ideal Toy Corp. Made in England under License by Ideal Toy Co. Ltd."

Stock Number: 4778-7
Item Name: ***Zeroid Action Set / Zerak***
Copyright Date: 1968
Contents:

Ideal Toys made two large boxed sets. They both included new accessories that were not originally available separately. The first of these sets was the *Zeroid Action Set*. This set came with any one of the first three robots, *Zintar*, *Zerak* or *Zobor*, which were randomly packaged. Also included in this set was one *Solar Cycle* and one *Missile Defense Pad*.

Accessories:

The accessories for this set included three missiles — one red, one blue and one yellow. Also included in this set were a yellow reversing ramp, and the standard additional *magnet*, *funnel* and *bomb*.

Packaging:

This piece was sold in a large white box with colorful stick on illustrations. The graphic illustrations, which are easily stained and torn, show *Zintar* in his *Solar Cycle*, while *Zerak* prepares to fire a missile from the launch ramp area. *Zobor* can be seen in the foreground preparing to fire a *bomb* from his *funnel* hand. Decals were not included with this set. The beige colored ramp was held in place, as was the lime green *Cycle*, by two card inserts. The *Zeroid* included with this set fit into a card insert designed specifically for the robot of choice. The complimentary accessory hands were provided.

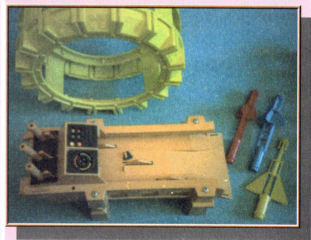

The *Zeroid Action Set*

Stock Number: 4779-5
Item Name: ***Zeroid Commander Action Set / Zogg***
Copyright Date: 1968
Contents:

This set was the most elaborate of the *Zeroid* sets. Unlike the generic sets that came before it, this set came only with *Commander Zogg*. This set was specially designed for *Zogg* in that he, through his

Dyno-Grid hands, could send battery power to accessory items, which enabled them to be spin and buzz.

Accessories:

This set included *Zogg* colored in green plastic, a *Solar Cycle* in lime green color, a *Sensor Station* molded in orange plastic with silver colored radar grid, and a *Sonic Alarm* molded in the color blue.

Packaging:

This was a huge box in comparison to other *Zeroid* packaging on the market at this time. Similar in design to the small *Zeroid Action Set*, this set, again, was a large white box with graphic-rich illustrations. Colorful illustrations of the *Sonic Alarm, Sensor Station* and *Solar Cycle* were shown. *Zogg* was highlight, and was clearly shown on the left-most part of the box. Inserts were used inside the box to hold all items. Decals were included for various panels — two for the *Sensor Station* and one for the *Sonic Alarm*. Hands were not included for *Zogg*, since his hands don't pull off as the other *Zeroids'* hands were designed to do.

The *Zeroid Commander Action Set*

Stock Number: 4649-0
Item Name: ***Missile Defense Pad***
Copyright Date: 1970
Contents:

During 1970, the same year that the *Zeroid Alien Invader* was introduced, Ideal Toys introduced the *Missile Defense Pad*, now molded in red plastic, as a separately boxed item. This toy was essentially to the previously released *Defense Pad* that was included in the *Commander Zogg Set*. This time around it was advertised as the *Multi-Rocket Launching System*. This set contained three missiles — yellow, blue and red — and the two piece red plastic molded ramp set. Also included were four leg supports.

Accessories:

None that although a *Zerak* robot is shown on the colorful box illustration, a *Zeroid* was not included with this boxed set.

Packaging:

The box is similar in philosophy to the *Alien* box. It's illustrated in bright purple and blue hues. The main title is written in block letters highlighted in bright yellow script.

Part 3 - *Mighty Zeroid Robots* and *STAR TEAM*

Stock Number: 4648-2
Item Name: **Sensor Station**
Copyright Date: 1970
Contents:

The *Sensor Station*, the "eyes and ears of the *Zeroid* complex" was sold in 1970 as a separate item. A few details had changed since it was introduced a year earlier as a means of communication, powered by and specifically for, *Commander Zogg*. The *Sensor Station* no longer required battery power to operate. The metal touch plates that transmitted power to the system from *Zogg's* two AA-size batteries had been replaced by a crank at the rear of the toy. By turning this crack, the radar and antenna grid would rotate. The metal grids had been remolded and now were simple plastic plate covers.

Accessories:

Included in this boxed set was a blue colored antenna and a red radar grid. An instruction sheet was included providing detailing information on such things as assembly, labels, hand operation and *Zeroid* ramp operation.

Packaging:

This box had the same measurements as the *Zeroid Missile Defense Pad*. Colorful illustration really made this box. The rear showed colored line drawings of *Zerak* (No. 4596-3), *Zobor* (No. 4597-1) and *Zintar* (No. 4662-3) with the tag line "Hey kids! Look for these additional *ZEROIDS* and accessories now available at your local dealer." It's interesting to note that, on this box back, Ideal Toys was not advertising the bubble carded *Zeroids*, as the production numbers listed above indicate. Illustrations of the three robots were *Zogg* (The Commander), then an illustration of the *Zeroid with Solar Cycle*, and *Missile*

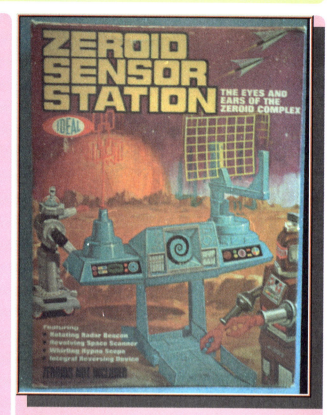

Defense Pad with script stating that "any *Zeroid* can climb up the ramp and automatically trigger the sequential firing of 3 harmless rockets . . . then with the flick of a lever he will back off." Finally *Zem XXI's* writers / designers commented that "Any *Zeroid* can be launched from this unique *Space Craft*. With a flip of a switch, the canopy turns as a eerie beeping is heard . . . the landing pads drop . . . the ramp is lowered and automatically the *Zeroid* leaves the craft."

STAR Team Toys 1977-1978 By Ideal Toys:

For one brief moment in time, *Zeroids* were reborn. It was an abomination of sorts, the last final gasp before death. The year was 1977, *Star Wars* had hit the screen and, by all standards, was a huge success, with toys flying off the shelves. Ideal Toys, seeing a perfect opportunity to make a quick profit revived the *Zeroids*, now renamed the *STAR TEAM*, one last and final time. If 1970 hadn't been bad enough, with those Kresges "Robots" and generic packing . . . 1977 was far worse. Gone were the *motorific* power plants that we loved so much . . . and in their place was nothing but a lump of blinking plastic. Rehashed names of former *Zeroids*, *Zem 21* now the name of a very *CP30*-looking robot, and the *Star Hawk* as a recasting of the original *Zem XXI*. A *Darth Vader* look-alike named the *Knight of Darkness*, and, of course, a human and his ship, *Kent*. Well, Kenner Toys and 20th Century Fox took a dim view of what they felt were copies of their now established toy lines. In the year 1978, they filed a lawsuit against Ideal. Surprisingly, the suit was later dropped. Ideal was able to prove that these were not in fact new toys. The designs, concepts and names had all been used previously. Perhaps this wasn't an infringement, as some have said, of the *Star Wars* franchise. Perhaps this was, for one last time, Ideal using their tremendous skill and ability in sensing the buying public's wants and needs, and yet again making a direct hit on the children's toy market. The *STAR TEAM* toys were popular, but alas, lived on for only one short year.

Stock Number: 4600-3
Item Name: **Zeroid**
Copyright Date: 1977
Contents:
   A *Zeroid* robot.
Accessories:
   This *Zeroid* robot didn't come with accessories items — no *Laser Beam*, no ramp, no *motorific* engine, and no *dyno* powered hands.
Packaging:
   Zeroid was sold separately and came in a brightly colored black and yellow, celo windowed box. Ideal toys exclaimed the virtues of the *Zeroid* "highly detailed action robot with moveable arms. *Zeroid* rolls on a moveable twin tread base. Flip on his special flashing lamp and send messages to his friends."

Stock Number: 4601-1
Item Name: **Zeroid and Star Hawk**
Copyright Date: 1977
Contents:
   The *Zeroid Star Hawk* was sold with a *Zeroid* robot.
Accessories:
   A decal sheet of exterior *Star Hawk* graphics was included with this boxed item.
Packaging:
   The *Star Hawk* was packaged in a smaller box than the original *ZEM XXI* ship. The *Star Hawk* was still dated with a 1970 copyright, as the first saucer was.

It, however, was produced for the 1977 line-up of *STAR TEAM* toys. This item was a direct copy of the original. Box graphics were a similar design concept showing the *Star Hawk* sitting on a blue lunarscaped planet. The hatch was open displaying a *Zeroid* robot inside. Note that the *Zeroid* was not the same as the original *Zeroid Robots*. The *Zeroid* was not driven by a *motorific* engine, and did not include a *Laser Beam*. However, it did have the arms of *Zogg*. There was no "head", but in its place was a dome, which lit when the toggle on the back of the robot was switched on. The line illustrations on the rear of the box state "*STAR HAWK* the spacecraft of the *Zeroid*. From one exciting adventure to another, Special motor opens the front hatch and lowers the landing pods."

Stock Number: 4602-9
Item Name: **Zem 21**
Copyright Date: 1977
Contents:
   Zem 21 was no longer the robot saucer ship of the 1970 line, but *Zem*'s name was reused. This time *Zem* was a very *CP30* looking 9" tall robot. His green headed and chromed body didn't come with accessory shoes or cloths.

Accessories:
 None.
Packaging:
 The new *Zem 21* came in a tall card box. The box had a large celo window that allowed the *Zem* to be viewed. The box was die cut unevenly and included a large black fin along the side. The celo window was trimmed in yellow with a large purple STAR TEAM logo. The box advertisement stated that "this metal plated humanoid robot can be posed in hundreds of positions. Create exciting action scenes with *Zem 21* and the other STAR TEAM figures."

Stock Number: 4603-7
Item Name: ***Knight of Darkness***
Copyright Date: 1977
Contents:
 Visions of the evil empire and *Darth Vader* must have entered children's minds in 1977. The *Knight of Darkness* was sold as a single item. Included with this item was his fierce looking *Laser Gun* and flowing black cape.
Accessories:
 The *Laser Gun* and cape accessorize the *Knight of Darkness*.
Packaging:
 This item was sold in a similar looking box to the somewhat shorter-boxed *Zem 21*. The large black celo windowed box permitted a clear view of this evil and powerful masked alien from the stars. Similar to the STAR HAWK, the rear illustration and text of this box stated that "The fearsome enemy of the ZEROIDS and ZEM 21, is a fully poseable figure and comes dressed in his special uniform and boots."

Stock Number: 4606-0
Item Name: ***Kent and Cosmic Cruiser***
Copyright Date: 1977
Contents:
 Kent was sold with his *Cosmic Cruiser*. A decal suit was included turning his *Cruiser* into a "real space vehicle."
Accessories:
 A large and detailed decal sheet was included. Also included with *Kent* was his red *Mork and Mindy*-looking space suit and red space helmet
Packaging:
 Kent and his *Cosmic Cruiser* were packaged in a very similar design to the STAR TEAM Zeroid and *Space Hawk*. The same flat black depiction of space was utilized. An illustration of *Kent* piloting the *Cruiser* was shown, with fire streaming out the rear "retro" rockets. Alien planets could be viewed, both in the top right corner of the box and to the lower left of the *Cruiser*.

Kent in his red *Mork and Mindy*-looking space suit and red space helmet

Part 3 - Mighty Zeroid Robots and STAR TEAM

Zeroid Robots And The Hong Kong Connection

As you've invariably figured out, *Zeroids* were made in many different box and packaging designs dependent on in which country the *Zeroid Robot* was to be sold. One of the most rare box designs, and thus scarce items, would have to be the *Zeroid Robots* that were produced for Asian Pacific Rim countries in the early 1970's. In fact, you, as a collector, have probably not heard of or seen this variation before. The *Zeroid Robots* were produced specifically for the Asian market near the end of their production run. The *Zeroid Robots* themselves were produced in Hong Kong by Ideal toys from the start to the end of production, but were only available for the export market.

The OK Company used a single box for all four *Zeroids*

Box artwork was significantly different than for the American market targeted *Zeroids*. There was only one box designed for all *Zeroids*. *Zerak*, *Zobor*, *Zintar* and *Zogg* were each packaged and sold separately. The generic box used for these four robots consisted of a clear cello wrap-around front window. The robot inside could be seen in full view. The *Zeroid* was attached to a white cardboard backing held in place with a white card base. There was no hard plastic utilized for the casing, as was common for most of the American packaging. The OK *Zeroid* window box was a simple throwaway container. The *Zeroids*' wrists were locked in place by pink twist tie wires. The exterior front of the box had written in English "Battery Operated Motor" at the bottom of the front. On the front of the box, in the upper-most area was written "*Zerak Robot*." It should noted that as all boxes were the same in design, photo art and text. Each box, regardless of which robot was included, was called the *Zerak Robot*, even though the *Zeroids* had their personal names embossed on their torsos. The top of the box lid was yellow with another *Zerak Robot* printed on it. The sides of the box showed a photo of *Zintar* overlaid on a moonscape with blue horizon. The rear of the box showed a similar *Zogg* and *Zobor*, again on the same lunarscape. The alternate side box artwork showed *Zerak* in an action pose hovering

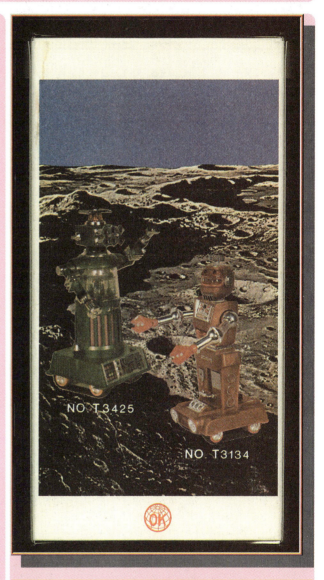

The back of the OK Company generic box

over another lunarscape with a blue horizon background. The rear of the box displayed the OK toy company logo. On the *Zerak* side of the box, at the lower right corner, was written "Made in Hong Kong." The exterior bottom of the box displayed a diagram for "assembly and operation." The two illustrations, interestingly enough, have a *Zogg* robot in the schematic

Asian *Zeroids* were inserted into their boxes on plain cardboard

Sides of the OK Company box and the generic instructions (below)

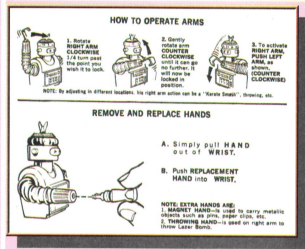

diagrams. A final note on the OK Company *Zeroids* is that, unlike the American supplied robots, these *Zeroids* did not come with additional "hands" or other accessories such as *bombs*. There were no yellow ramps included, nor separate instruction sheets. OK *Zeroids* were produced only for the Hong Kong and Asian markets. There were no plans to, nor did OK, export

them throughout the rest of the world. They exist in extremely limited quantities in Canada and the United States only through the importing of collectors and travelers who have purchased them abroad.

Enter The Five And Dime

The Ideal Toy Company saw a dramatic decline in the sales of their once *Mighty Zeroid Robots* in the early part of the 1970's. Boys and girls had become bored with the notion of space exploration and travel. NASA missions were becoming tedious, and the public in general felt that space travel had become safe and commonplace. The successes and heroics of the space program, and its experiments that would pave the way for future vaccines and provide a greater understanding of the effects of humans living in space, was receiving less and less coverage on the evening news. In many cases, space related news had moved from the front pages of national newspapers.

What to do? Ideal, looking to increase their profit margin, (by selling more toys with the smallest investment of capital) moved from producing *Zeroid Robots* in their elaborate plastic containers to much cheaper packaging. Gone were the beautifully illustrated card sleeves and header cards. Packaging of the *Zeroid Robots* had been, from the word go, an evolution in packaging and cost effectiveness and efficiency.

Part 3 - *Mighty Zeroid Robots* and *STAR TEAM*

Sleeve Packaging

The *Mighty Zeroid Robots* for the Christmas 1967 had been packaged in beautifully illustrated sleeve boxes. These boxes, which are, as with many *Zeroid* robot items, extremely hard to find, are rare as a result of their fragility. I've included sleeve pictures here for your information. The plastic plexi-glass case and robot fit inside the sleeve which was illustrated with the *Zeroid Robot* packaged inside. The front of the box artwork was colored in bright red for *Zintar*, light green for *Zobor*, and purple for *Zobor*. The left side of each box showed through artist illustrations from top to bottom.

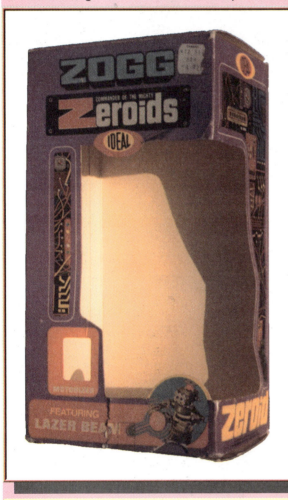

A rare sleeve box

Each *Zeroid* was pictured with his accessory case "working action feature." Next, was pictured a *Zeroid* with an outstretched arm with the caption "use magnetic hand to carry metallic objects." And finally, the bottom illustration showed an artist's concept of the *Zeroid* under power with the caption "runs forward and backward." The right side of the box used similar type illustrations with the captioning "set arm to perform karate smash" and "set arm to launch satellite." Both the box lid and box bottom for each *Zeroid* contained

Back of a sleeve box

the name of the *Zeroid*, such as *Zintar of the Mighty Zeroids*, with a large colorful Ideal logo and product number. The backside of each box was highly detailed and was an exact duplicate of the later header cards that replaced the sleeve boxing. This replacement of the boxing occurred almost immediately after production had begun on *Zeroids*. As it happened, the *Zeroid* packaging was being damaged in shipping and, as a result, 1968 saw the introduction of a new "header card" replacing the original sleeve designed boxes.

Header Carded Packaging

Ideal did continue to use the plastic cases and play station notion. The new header cards were a much simpler, less costly design than the original elaborate packaging. In this incarnation, the header cards clipped onto six small pegs on the back of the molded colored case. Tape was always used to ensure that the header

A header carded *Zerak*

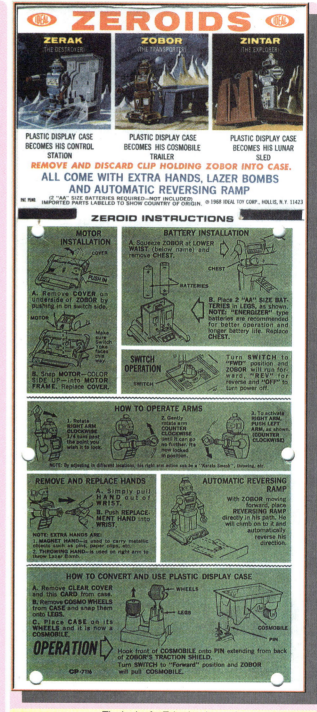

The back of a *Zobor* header card

cards didn't come off. You won't find a *Zeroid* case that hasn't had the header card taped on, because that was factory practice. The header card itself towers above the case by about 4". The header card text design is similar for all robots. All include the *Zeroid's* name in large bold print in the uppermost left corner. In small block print underneath, the name is written, "of the mighty", and then, in very large yellow text, is the word *Zeroids*. Each card face has an illustration of an alien landscape with mountains and cliffs in the foreground. The illustrations are not the same on close examination. *Zerak's* illustration is of blue hued peaks and valley's with a ringed planet on the lower left of the card. *Zintar's* illustration includes sand colored terrain with tall mountains and two very small planets in the midnight sky. *Zintar* is illustrated operating his *Sled* over the surface. *Zobor's* header illustration is of the robot

pulling his *Cosmobile* across a green planetoid and a blue, earth-like planet is rising over the heavily shadowed peaks. Each *Zeroid* card includes the Ideal logo written in blue with white oval and red background on the front of the header card. A product number is included to the far lower right. The rear of the boxes contained highly detailed information about the operation of the *Zeroid Robot* inside the case. The rear of the header cards were not generic instructions. Specific diagrams show such things as motor

Part 3 - Mighty Zeroid Robots and STAR TEAM

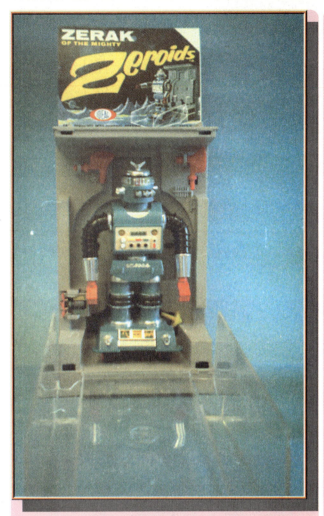

An open header carded *Zerak* showing mounted accessories

of all the plexi-glass *Zeroid* boxes — they are stackable. I recall as a child going with my mother into the local Simpson-Sears store, and, in the toy section of the store, *Zeroid Robots* could be found stacked on top of each other. The header card design and small runners that were included on both the top and the bottom of the boxes allowed other *Zeroid* boxes to be "locked" in these sliders for ease of display.

Bubble Carded Packaging

In 1970 Ideal added to the line of *Zeroid Robots* and again changed their packaging. The 1970 product catalogue confirms that *Zerak* (product number 4596-3), *Zobor* (4597-1) and *Zintar* (4662-3) could now be purchased on bubble cards. Potential buyers could order *Zeroids* in one dozen allotments. The merchandising catalogue stated about the new packaging "Our three basic *Zeroids* in new, blister packages. Each packed with a *Laser Bomb* and extra pair of utility hands that can throw, pull, push and haul. *Zeroids* can move forward or backward on their treads. 2 "AA" size batteries required (not included)." The artwork on the new, large bubble card had changed conceptionally from the original *Zeroid* cards. The coloring was now new and flashy. Lime green, purple and pink were the base colors. This theme, incidentally, was reflected in other *Zeroids* packaging at the time. The *Command Set* pieces were now sold separately, and box illustrations were more futuristic and cartoonish

installation, battery installation, and switch operation. There was a section on how to operate the arms, remove and replace the hands, the automatic reversing ramp, and how to convert and use the specific *Zeroid* display case. Included with each of the *Zeroids* were, of course, their accessory "hands" and a *bomb*, as well as the yellow *Zeroid* ramp. There are two types of ramps. One type didn't have *Zeroids* in black paint embossed on the "front" of the ramp. This was the ramp that was included with the two *Action Sets*. The ramp that did have the word *Zeroid* was included in the plexi-glass-cased version, and in both *Zintar* and *Zobor* could be seen though their clear case covers. The *Zerak* case also included the ramp inside the box. It couldn't be seen however. A notable variation in the *Zerak* boxing is a case includes the word *Zeroid* embossed onto the lower section of the gray case, underneath the hinged ramp. I also have a *Zerak* in the same box, complete with no variations, other than that the box is without the embossing. It's an interesting variation in as much as the *Zeroid* word is not just printed on the box, but the box has been molded with these letters protuberant and highlighted in yellow. One final note on the design

A bubble carded *Zerak* with no accessories

Part 3 - Mighty Zeroid Robots and STAR TEAM

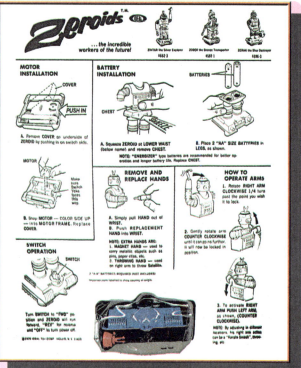

The back of a bubble carded *Zerak* with generic instructions

Generic Packaging

Welcome to the five and dime *Zerak*, *Zogg*, *Zemo*, *Zobor* and *Zintar*. All five robots were sold in their final box variation through "five and dime" stores. This was the last variation of *Zeroids*' boxing, and the death knell for the toys in general. As with the OK Company, Ideal saw fit to sell the license for *Zeroid Robots*, which resulted in their packaging deteriorating to a less costly, plain white, generic window box to supply the five and dime stores. The *Zeroids* themselves hadn't changed from their initial design of a few years earlier. They were still powered by their *motorific* engines and came with their accessory "hands" and *bombs*, but less their reversing ramps. The boxing for the *Zeroids*, as you'll see in the pictures, is a plain, off white, soft card box. It's not the same high gloss finished card used for the OK Company packaging. The exterior of the box was printed in a non-gloss blue ink with a crude illustration of a *Zeroid*.

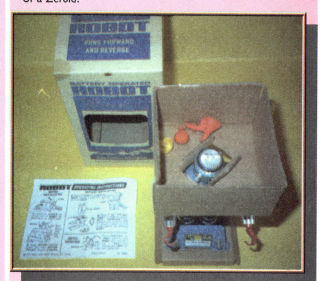

The low cost generic boxing of Zeroids

looking. Pink, purple and lime green were definitely the "in" colors at the time. Gone was the dark coloring of the mid-1960's. The *Alien Invader* and *ZEM XXI* reflected the same design them as they were molded in the bright pinks and purples. The carded *Zeroids* were a definite money saver for Ideal. First of all, no plastics were used for the casing — colorful cardboard and a molded bubble provided the packaging. The yellow ramp was no longer available. The *motorific* engine was still provided and was attached to the card by a bubble. The header card now stated "*Zeroids* . . . mighty machines from outer space." The colorful illustration depicted *Zintar*, *Zobor* and *Zerak* traversing a blue, crater strewn landscape. *Zobor* could be seen in the foreground inside his *Solar Cycle*. The *Zem XXI* was now depicted in illustrations. The front of the card, to the left and right of the *Zeroid Robot*, depicted all three robots in action — *Zintar* carrying a *motorific* engine, *Zerak* chopping and running in forward motion, and *Zobor* firing missiles. These four yellow background illustrations were striking on their navy blue card. The rear of the card was now generic, illustrating the basic instructions for the operation and battery installation of all three robots. Nowhere on the card was it specified which *Zeroid Robot* the card was for — sort of a one-size-fits-all — costs for printing were cut since one card was now used for all. These cards are, for obvious reasons, virtually impossible to locate. If the *Zeroids* were played with, then the cards were destroyed, since the bubbles were not removable, but glued to the outer surface of the card.

If you look closely at the illustration however, the *Zeroid* shown is not one of the known *Zeroid* designs at all. This *Zeroid* illustration is made up of a *Zemo* head and arms with a *Zintar* torso and base. It's a crude picture at best, and isn't to scale with the real life *Zeroids*. Manufacturing of the *Zeroids* continued in Hong Kong, but the new, basic boxes were now printed in the USA and Manufactured for "S.S. Kresge Company, Detroit, Michigan 48232." The exterior of the box simply stated "Battery Operated Robot — runs forward and reverse." On the front of the box, a small window had been die cut so that the robot inside could be viewed. The exterior of the box didn't identify which *Zeroid* you would be buying, since they had now become "ROBOTS" and were not, in fact, identified as *Zeroids* any longer. "Imported parts labeled to show country of

Part 3 - Mighty Zeroid Robots and STAR TEAM

Only Zogg peeking out the hole tells you who's inside

labeled "Ideal Toy Corp., Hollis, N.Y. 11423, 2L-0221." The instruction sheet included with the robots didn't identify them as *Zeroid Robots* either. It was a double-sided instruction sheet simply labeled "Robot operating instructions." Of note is that the diagrams shown were taken directly from the much earlier original sleeve boxed artwork by Ideal toys. Robots in the Kresge five and dime boxes are significantly harder to come by than the plexi-glass case versions produced earlier. They will always command higher prices because of the poor quality card boxes, which rarely have survived intact for the past thirty years.

One final note on the decline of interest and the cost cutting associated with the *Zeroid Robots* — it's interesting to review Ideal Toys pricing and toy packaging strategies. The original *Zeroid Robots* (1968) were packaged in their cardboard outer sleeved plastic boxes with plastic clear cover. That same year, *Zeroids* were re-packaged with new header cards since there was concern expressed over the damaged "sleeve" boxes that were arriving at toy stores and outlets. By 1970, the *Zeroids* were being repackaged on their new bubble cards since this represented a significant cost saving for Ideal Toys. The bubble cards were certainly far cheaper to manufacture — less material (plastic was out) — and generic boxes were in. By 1971, Ideal had sold the licensing rights for the *Zeroid Robots* and they were yet again repackaged, this time for Kresges department (Five and Dime) stores, which later became K Mart. At this time, *Zeroids* were also repackaged for the Asian market, boxed in the OK Company packaging. The *Zeroid Robots* toys themselves were not changed from their original design, and, right to the end of manufacture, the black base plate on the bottom on every *Zeroid* read "1968 Ideal, Hong Kong." The once great *Zeroid Robots*, which had retailed for between $3.99 and $4.99 in their original plastic playset cases, were eventually sold through Kresges five and dime stores for a mere 68 cents.

origin" was printed in the lower front of the box. Inside the box was a manila cardboard base plate that supported the base / treads of the robot. The "head" of the robot was held in place by a similar cardboard support with "hand" accessories sitting loosely in this card shelf. The instruction sheet was dated 1971 and

Zeroid And STAR Team Price Guide

As with the *Matt Mason* section of this guide, I'm sure that you'll find this price section controversial and will disagree with some of the prices. It's my hope that you'll also find pricing that will surprise you. *Mighty Zeroid Robots* and, to a lesser extent *STAR Team* toys, have seen tremendous growth in collectability over the last few years, and prices continue to rise very rapidly. Because of the fragility of the robots themselves, and the aging of plastics (including the plexi-glass casing) as opposed to their rubber compound counterparts (such as *Major Matt Mason*), robots are almost impossible to find complete and boxed. The prices in this section were as accurate as possible at the time of going to press. The *Zeroid* and *STAR Team* toy values presented in this reference guide are based on years of collecting and speaking with numerous collectors and dealers worldwide, as well as what I, as a collector, have paid for a particular toy. The prices that are shown reflect the current prices that you can expect to pay for a *Zeroid Robot* or *STAR Team* toy. As with the values in the *Major Matt Mason* section, values here are based on dealer asking prices at toy shows, and from printed sources such as toy collectable publications and mail order. As with any collectable item, the value is directly related to the intrinsic value that a prospective collector places on the item.

There are always going to be times when you stumble across a toy which should command a high price, but is priced low, or vise versa. One such time occurred while I was on a trip visiting friends in Ireland. As it happened, three friends and myself were traveling from Dublin to County Cork and happen upon a number of very picturesque and quaint villages (where we had to stop and take pictures.) In one village, I don't recall the name now, I found a very old local toy and hobby shop. On entering the shop, I discovered dozens of pieces of old toy stock from the late 1960's and early 1970's. I struck up a friendly conversation with the elderly husband and wife owners who were more than happy to allow me into their storage room to look at the "old unsold junk." The "old junk", which they were anxious to be rid of, consisted of perfectly preserved items such as Bendie *Batmans*, Corgi *Batmobiles*, *James Bond* cars, Mattel *Thingmakers*, *SSP*'s and *Mighty Zeroid Robots*. I left the store with three hockey size duffel bags full of toys! That began my quest for *Zeroid Robots*. They had been, up to that point, a long forgotten childhood toy.

Supply and demand are most often the determining factors for pricing any collectable toy, along with the second most important price factor, complete and original boxes, packaging and instructions. This price section includes the box or carded value of the toy. In the *Zeroid Robot* section specifically, I'll include pricing for *Zeroids* that are in their plexi-glass cases, but incomplete without their header cards. *Zeroids*, when found boxed at all, will most often be incomplete without header or sleeve cards. Such a *Zeroid* would obviously command less than a header carded case, but more than a loose toy. Because there are only color variations among the *Zeroid Robots* (other than packaging) or *Star Team* toys, they'll be priced separately as well. When the toy item is described as loose I'm referring to an item that isn't boxed or carded, but is complete. These toys will be included at the end of the value section. The first price provided will be for a boxed toy in mint / like new condition. It should be noted that, if a toy box or card is torn, worn, missing, or doesn't have its inner packing or decals, it's not complete or mint. In the real world, it shouldn't demand the maximum price, but rather should fall in the price range between a loose and mint in boxed item. It's always, as I stated before, the discretion of the buyer and the willingness of the seller that determine an agreeable amount for a particular toy. The prices that I've provided in this reference guide are the prices that you should expect to pay to buy an item. They're not necessarily what you can expect to receive when you're selling the same toy to a toy dealer — in fact, you should expect only about fifty percent of the guide price when selling to a dealer. Finally, the prices provided here are based on United States currency.

Zeroid Robots and STAR Team Values

How To Use Zeroid Robots and STAR Team Reference Guide

The following pages identify toys using the original Ideal Company stock numbers for the *Zeroid Robots* and *Star Team* toys and the official figure or accessory name. For each toy a Mint Boxed, MOC (Mint on Card) or loose value where applicable, is given, and the MIMB (Mint in Mint Box) value of each toy (excluding loose toys) is listed to the right. In this instance, Mint Boxed refers to the item being boxed, but not complete with the header card or sleeve. The MIMB *Zeroid Robot* will be complete with the header card or sleeve. I have included values for toys that are either off the card or out of the box, and toys that were not originally packaged separately, but which can be found as single items.

Zeroids: Ideal Toys 1967 – 1970

Plexi-Glass Case With Header Card Insert By Ideal Toys

Stock Number	Item Name	Mint Boxed	MIMB
4773-8	*Zintar*	175.00	275.00
4772-0	*Zobor*	150.00	250.00
4771-2	*Zerak*	200.00	275.00

Part 3 - Mighty Zeroid Robots and STAR Team

Plexi-Glass Case With Outer Sleeve Insert By Ideal Toys

Stock Number	Item Name	Mint Boxed	MIMB
4773-8	*Zintar*	175.00	350.00
4772-0	*Zobor*	150.00	325.00
4771-8	*Zerak*	200.00	350.00
4763-9	*Zogg*	400.00	500.00

Blister Packs By Ideal Toys

Stock Number	Item Name	MOC
4662-3	*Zintar*	400.00
4597-1	*Zobor*	350.00
4596-3	*Zerak*	400.00

S.S. Kresge Company By Ideal Toys

Stock Number	Item Name	MIMB
4777-9	*Zintar* (gray)	250.00
4777-9	*Zobor*	225.00
4777-9	*Zerak*	250.00
4777-9	*Zogg*	350.00
4777-9	*Zemo*	500.00

OK Company, Hong Kong By Ideal Toys

Stock Number	Item Name	MIMB
T3135	*Zintar*	400.00
T3134	*Zobor*	400.00
T3133	*Zerak*	400.00
T3425	*Zogg*	500.00

★ ZEROIDS IN BLISTER PACK

Zogg's laser beam

Zeroids And Accessories By Ideal Toys

Stock Number	Item Name	MIMB
4608-6	*ZEM XXI Zeroid Explorer Module*	400.00
4659-9	*Alien Invader*	400.00
4764-7	*Zeroid with Solar Cycle / Zintar*	350.00
4764-7	*Zeroid with Solar Cycle / Zobor*	300.00
4764-7	*Zeroid with Solar Cycle / Zerak*	350.00
4778-7	*Zeroid Action Set / Zintar*	300.00
4778-7	*Zeroid Action Set / Zobor*	275.00
4778-7	*Zeroid Action Set / Zerak*	300.00
4779-5	*Zeroid Commander Action Set / Zogg*	350.00
4649-0	*Missile Defense Pad*	275.00
4648-2	*Sensor Station*	250.00

Loose Zeroid Robots And Accessory Values

Item Name	Loose Value	Complete Value
Zintar (gray)	50.00	100.00
Zintar (silver)	50.00	100.00
Zerak	50.00	100.00
Zobor	40.00	90.00
Zogg	60.00	110.00
Zemo (red)	100.00	400.00

Part 3 - Mighty Zeroid Robots and STAR TEAM

Loose Zeroid Robots And Accessory Values (continued)

Zemo (aqua)	100.00	400.00
Zeroid Alien	40.00	125.00
Solar Cycle	N/A	40.00
Missile Defense Pad	N/A	85.00
Missiles	N/A	15.00
Sensor Station	N/A	75.00
Zogg's Laser Beam	N/A	40.00
Zem XXI	N/A	200.00
Miscellaneous hands	N/A	10.00
Motorific Motors	N/A	20.00
Yellow Ramps	N/A	10.00

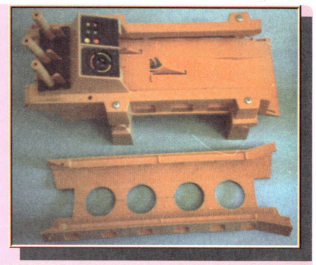

Missile Launch Pad from the *Zeroid Action Set*

Zeroid Commander Action Set

Part 3 - *Mighty Zeroid Robots* and *STAR TEAM*

STAR TEAM Toys 1969–1970 By Ideal Toys

Item Name	Loose Value	MIMB
Space Belt Set *	N/A	55.00
Space Helmet	25.00	95.00
Space Boots	20.00	75.00
Nebulizer Gun	25.00	45.00
Remote Gripper	25.00	45.00

* includes child's size utility belt, gravity tool, communicator, scope and life support.

STAR TEAM Toys 1977 – 1978 By Ideal Toys

Stock Number	Item Name	Loose Value	MIMB
4600-3	Zeroid	10.00	25.00
4601-1	Zeroid and Star Hawk	25.00	75.00
4602-9	Zem 21	15.00	45.00
4603-7	Knight of Darkness	20.00	45.00
4606-0	Kent and Cosmic Cruiser	50.00	75.00

Part 3 - Mighty Zeroid Robots and STAR TEAM

Toy Variations, Knock-Offs And Prototypes

The Knock-Offs

Following the releasing to the buying public of Ideal Toys *motorific terrific Zeroids*, numerous other toy companies made attempts to cash in on a very successful franchise. Copies of the *Zeroids* began turning up almost immediately in the early half of the 1970's. These unlicensed toy companies made almost exact duplicates of *Zeroids*. A prime example would be the look-alike wind-up *Zeroid* toys of Durham. This company put out three robots that bore a remarkable resemblance to *Zeroids*. These were not battery powered as the *Zeroids* were, but rather wind-ups. They were sold on bubble cards, not unlike the 1970 *Zeroids*. True, they are not a *Zeroid*, but they are rare and highly sought after, especially in their unique packaging. Another *Zeroid* look-alike was made by Imperial. These 5" tall rubber bendies, of which two were made, bore a striking resemblance as well. They're not particularity rare, nor are they expensive. Both versions of these rubber robots can be had, packaged, for about $25.00 or less. Did you know there's another *Zeroid*-type rip-off — a remote control robot with wired stop and go motion? This item is rare and difficult to find, especially packaged.

Wind up robot from Durham that very much resembles the *Zeroids*

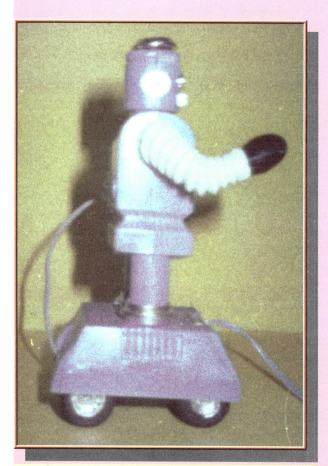

Remote controlled robot (above and right) in the *Zeroid* style

This rubber robot from Imperial could be *Zintar's* cousin

Two of three Imperial *Space Fighter* robots look like *Zeroids*

The Variations

Unlike *Major Matt Mason* toys, *Zeroid Robots* don't have variations, except one — packaging was changed many times, as noted above, but the *Zeroid Robots* themselves, *Zintar*, *Zobor*, *Zerak*, *Zogg* and *Zemo* were not. There is only one known variation, that being *Zintar*. It would appear that somewhere in the production life of this robot, the plastic used for the body molds was changed. *Zintar* can be found most often in his standard gray colored plastic. There is a variation, which I have in my own collection, pictured here. This variation is the same mold as used for the gray *Zintar*, But differs in the color of the robot. The plastic takes on an almost pearl-type color and texturing, not dissimilar to the texture of *Zobor*.

The Prototypes

The 1970 Ideal Toys catalogue displayed numerous *Zeroid* toys, from a sleeve boxed *Zogg* to bubble carded *Zeroids*. What's significant and interesting to note is the number of prototypes that are included on those Ideal Toy pages. Prototypes most often occur when toy companies don't have the final "product" ready for the market. Since catalogues can come into being very much in advance of a new toy line, prototype photographs may be used to gage buyer approval for a new line. The *Zeroid Robots* were no strangers to prototypes and, in fact, the 1970 catalogue specifically shows a number of them. Before you go out looking for

prototypes, it's important to realize that most prototypes exist in very limited quantities, usually fewer than ten. I've included many prototype pictures for your information. For instance, you'll notice that the box artwork that's shown for *Zerak*, *Zobor* and *Zintar* located on page 29 of the Ideal catalogue clearly shows prototype box art. If you look closely you'll see that box design and coloring reflect the production market versions, however the "Z" in *Zeroids* on the front of the box is stylized. The "Z" that was used for the actual box is a straight edged and bold type set "Z". Further prototypes are shown on page 31. Note that the box art shown is highly stylized. Ideal Toys didn't go with the large *Zeroid* lettering that has a definite curvature. The *Zeroid Action Set* printing is, in reality, square and balanced on the production box. Other changes include different color box art. The color of the box over the graphic area is white using blue and red blocked lettering. The prototype however shows a solid yellow foreground. The alien terrain illustration is the same as the finalized box version, and the variations continue . . . The *Sonic Siren* wasn't chromed, but the catalogue shows a red siren with a chromed speaker nozzle. Another variation is the chromed radar dish and antenna on the *Sensor Station*. The console appears to include more detailed controls than on the final production version as well. A final note is on the "ramps" of both the *Sonic Alarm* and *Sensor Station* in which the grating on the ramp tracks has taken on a more detailed and authentic grating effect, more so than the final toy designs do. The Ideal catalogue shows some minor box artwork changes as well. Just as *Major Matt Mason* had minor but numerous changes, so did Ideal. The *Zem XXI* ship box's original concept was a blue planetoid surface with a similar blue hued sky with the *Zem* logo printed in yellow. This was, of course, changed to a more dramatic pink and yellow illustration with yellow and lime green script, keeping with the new colors for 1970 production. The *Alien* box too originally had totally different art work. The production box has the name of the *Zeroid* straight across the top of the box, with the *Invader* entering from the left side. The original concept box illustration showed the same pink hued sky, however the landscape was similar to the *Zem XXI* prototype, which was blue in color. This was later changed to a reddish brown planetscape for final production. Lastly, the original title for the box, while using the same text and script, was printed on a diagonal, with the left top corner of the box being the center point of the script.

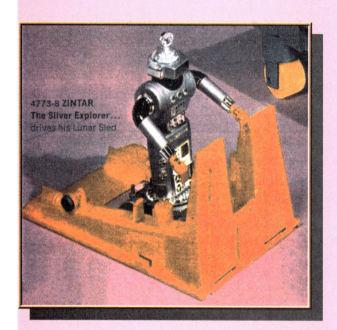

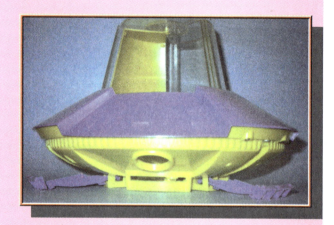

Zintar, Zobor, ZEM XXI and Zemo

Part 3 - Mighty Zeroid Robots and STAR TEAM

19   **TOYS**

ZEM 21® `TV`
4602-9
Zem 21 stands 9" tall, he's fully poseable, and his jointed humanoid body is designed with all the mechanical chrome styling of a real super-science robot of tomorrow. He's not a leader, though—he needs a Zeroid companion to do his thinking for him. But what an action pair Zem 21 and Zeroid make together!
Pack: 12 pcs. Wgt: 11 lbs.

KNIGHT OF DARKNESS® `TV`
4603-7
Ideal's Knight of Darkness: somber, powerful, an 11½" fully poseable figure in imperial black cape, black and silver uniform, with a grim masked head that strikes terror into the bravest heart!
In his hand, a futuristic weapon. Black boots, black hands complete his menacing appearance. The Knight of Darkness—perfect bad guy for long hours of imagination and excitement.
Pack: 12 pcs. Wgt: 14 lbs.

ZEROID® `TV`
4600-3
Zeroids are sold separately, too—a perfect way for kids to add to their Star Team strength.
Individual Zeroids have blue accents and stripes.
With more than one Zeroid to share the brainwork, the Star Team has an even better chance against the Knight of Darkness! (2 AA batteries not included.)
Pack: 12 pcs. Wgt: 11 lbs.

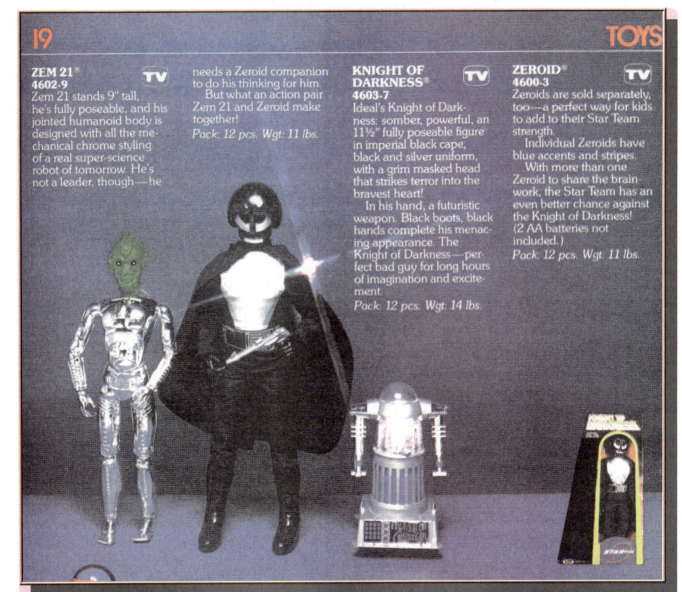

KENT AND HIS COSMIC CRUISER™ `TV`
4606-0
Here's the space hero every kid can identify with ...and the star cruiser that can take him on missions to the far reaches of the galaxy!
Kent stands 9" tall, blasts through space in his Cosmic Cruiser or leaves his vehicle for adventures on distant planets. He's fully poseable, with Star Team coverall uniform and helmet.
The Cosmic Cruiser looks like a real space vehicle: blunt nose for re-entry, computer control panel, authentic Star Team insignia and markings, with wheels for push play action on any surface.
Kent and his Cosmic Cruiser...Ideal's Star Team leader in the space race of '78!
Pack: 6 pcs. Wgt: 11 lbs.

Part 3 - *Mighty Zeroid Robots* and *STAR TEAM*

18

STAR TEAM® WINS THE SPACE RACE!

Star Team, from Ideal—fantastic action figures that bring the future down to earth today. Stalwart heroes, menacing villains, lovable robots and space vehicles that conquer the space system.

Join the Star Team...let Ideal help you capture all the sellout demand created by the science fiction boom!

ZEROID® AND STAR HAWK™　4601-1 TV

The original Star Team robot and starship!

Zeroid is a friendly, intelligent 5½" tall robot with red accent stripes, moveable arms, rubber treads and a blinking light in his head that shows his brain is working full time. He's loveable, but he's got the key strategies the Star Team needs to defeat the Knight of Darkness.

His Star Hawk is 14" in diameter, a super interplanetary vehicle with transparent cockpit dome, computer instrument panel, three pods for landing, a mechanical airlock door that makes a wierd outer-space sound when it opens, even a retractable ramp for Zeroid to disembark. Open the door, and legs and ramp extend automatically.

Zeroid and Star Hawk...super members of Ideal's Star Team! (Some assembly required: 2 AA batteries not included.) *Pack: 4 pcs. Wgt. 20 lbs.*

The *STAR TEAM*'s *Star Hawk* is a *ZEM XXI* with new colors

Part 3 - Mighty Zeroid Robots and STAR TEAM

Colorform Toys
OUTER SPACE MEN

Outer Space Men (Colorforms Toy Company)

Prelude - First Contact

The following pages of this book are special and dedicated to all those boys and girls who played with the *Outer Space Men* from 1968 through 1970. These pages review this most unique and fascinating line of bendie-type toys with colorful photographs and imaginative descriptors straight from the box artwork. It will chronicle the interesting development of the most intriguing science fiction alien space toy line of all time. Here, you will meet the most imaginatively designed seven aliens to come out of the 1960's toy industry. This seven piece set includes *Commander Comet – The Man from Venus, Alpha 7 – The Man from Mars, Colossus Rex – The Man from Jupiter, Electron+ - The Man from Pluto, Astro-Nautilus – The Man from Neptune, Xodiac – The Man from Saturn* and *Orbitron – The Man from Uranus*. The *Outer Space Men*, from Colorforms, filled the alien gap left by the *Major Matt Mason* line of toys by Mattel. We had the Mattel bendie astronauts heading off into unknown alien space adventures with their friends *Scorpio* and *Callisto* but, when these brave astronauts landed on the planets of our solar system, what did they find? Colorforms had us believe that, perhaps, there might just be aliens waiting, and they had seven of them ready to meet any human threat or adventure. The galaxy was beginning to become a pretty crowded place in the late 1960's. *Zeroids* where hanging out on planet *Zero* too. Would they head to our solar system flying aboard the *ZEM XXI* ?

The original seven Colorforms *Outer Space Men*

Colorforms manufactured their "Men" for only a few short years. In some foreign markets, this line of toys was manufactured in other formats. This guide will identify all known copies of the *Outer Space Men* — and there were many. These unlicensed toys were sold in a variety of packaging types, and in a number of different sizes and materials. As with both the *Major Matt Mason* line of toys and the *Mighty Zeroids Robots*, Colorforms *Outer Space Men* continue to be found in new and interesting variations, so this can not be the definitive guide to these toys, although it does cover all of Colorforms' known production, all of which was in the United States, Canada and the Asian markets.

Colorforms - Three Dimensional Catch-Up
The *Outer Space Men* - In The Beginning . . . .

. . . there was the Colorform company, who, in the later half of the 1950's through the 1960's, made wonderful Colorform rub-ons, in card board and then vinyl stick-on transfers for myriad subjects including the 1959 *Popeye the Weatherman* Colorforms, the 1962 *Miss Ballerina Dress-Up Kit*, and the 1966 *Batman Print Putty*. Many a rainy day saw children entertaining themselves for hours with these wonderful and imaginative activities and their colorful artwork. Of course, not missed by any toy company including Colorforms, was the incredible interest in space and particularly the US space program, once it was known that the Soviet Union had reached earth orbit first in 1957 with their tiny *Sputnik*. Real life drama was unfolding regularly in front of the American public on the nightly news. The testing of new and larger rocket booster engines, new and improved space suit designs, discussions of further missions to the moon, Mars and beyond were commonplace, both on the television and in the classroom. *Star Trek* hit the airwaves in the mid-1960's, and showed an optimistic and hopeful future. Ships would voyage to the stars and meet all kinds of alien civilizations, some friendly some not so. The Colorform Company, very much aware of the space phenomenon, began design discussions about creating their own line of space toys. This three-dimensional line would not compete with *Major Matt Mason's Man in Space* line from Mattel. Rather, the Colorform Company toy designs would compliment *Major Matt Mason* and his space fairing human friends. Colorforms decided instead to launch into space and the science fiction world with their *Outer Space Men*. These wild looking seven figures were designed by Mel Birnkrant, who was, at the time, a toy designer and free lance writer. Birnkrant was responsible for coming up with the very imaginative bubble box artwork, since he was not only the creator of the Colorforms, but was the Art Director for this series of toys as well. These figures, designed and named after all the planets in our solar system except for Mercury, each displayed on his box a large collection of scientific facts concerning the planet from which he heralded. The design of the toy was tied to the nature and mythos of each planet — the angel from the planet Venus, little green man from Mars, etc. A combination of fact and fantasy intertwined into an exciting new alien space toy. Colorform rode high on the excitement and enthusiasm for the *Outer Space Men*. They were a huge success,

The *Outer Space Men* complemented Mattel's *Man In Space* figures

and the public clamored for a second series. The designs were again handled by Mel Birnkrant, and the new *Outer Space Men*, now renamed as the very catchy "World of the Future" figures, were readied to premier at the 1969 New York Toy Fair. It must have been fate — the toys never did make it to the show because of an unfortunate mix up in shipping, and, as Mattel and Ideal were finding with their space toys, interest in space was waning. On July 20, 1969, Neil Armstrong was the first to walk on the face of another celestial body. The moon now seemed a whole lot closer, and those flickering black and white transmissions watched on television sets around the world didn't look like the colorful and imaginative worlds painted by Colorforms. Stark gray dust, flat expansions, dust, crater pocked surfaces, and lunar rock destroyed the fantasy world of the Colorform aliens. And where were the aliens? The moon was a barren wasteland, long dead. Series two, *The World of the Future*, was canceled shortly after the most historic event in mankind's history, setting foot on the moon, took place. The *World of the Future* never reached fruition, and only a handful of prototype aliens and cards exist — a sad commentary on a once mighty line of toys. Colorforms soon had company, with *Major Matt Mason* and *Zeroid Robots* following in its footsteps. *Major Matt Mason* may have been the hero of the toy space program, but Colorforms were definitely the imagination champ. To this day, their designs and imaginative box artwork is unsurpassed.

The Outer Space Men Product Line

The first set and only official set of Colorform aliens was produced in the late 1960's. The product line was made up of a total of seven bendie-type figures. These figures, as with the *Major Matt Mason* line of toys, were made of a pliable rubber compound molded over a wire metal skeletal framework. The wires seem to have held up well in many cases, and appear to be of better quality than the *Major Matt Mason* line that it attempted to emulate. Similar to the *Matt Mason* line however, there is a chemical interaction that occurs between some of the hard plastics and the rubber body compound, resulting in some melting of accessories such as helmets. Often times for example *Xodiac, the Man from Saturn* can be found with melt marks in his helmet where his ears touched the harder plastic helmet material. The seven *Outer Space Men* figures were conceived as extra-terrestrial life forms living within our solar system, excluding the planets Earth and Mercury. In the first series of toys, all figures were sold with accessories, such as *ray gun* weapons, maces, helmets and *cosmic staffs*. *Outer Space Men* were advertised as "Flexible Space Figures" that could "Bend to Thousands of Action Positions" and were "complete with weapon." Each figure, regardless of its size — and they ranged from as small as 3" to as tall as 6" — was sold on an 8" x 10" bubbled, highly informational, and beautifully illustrated display card.

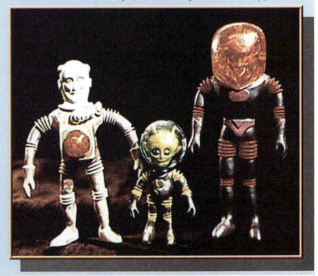

Electron+, Alpha 7 and *Xodiac*

Item Name: **Alpha 7 – The Man from Mars**
Copyright Date: 1968
Accessories: *Ray Gun* and *Space Helmet*.
Details:

Alpha 7 was a very small (about 3" tall) alien with a green head and blue painted body. His joints, similar to *Major Matt Mason's* accordion joints, remained unpainted from the factory. The rubber used to mold *Alpha 7* was bright lime green in color and a soft flexible rubber. This alien *Man from Mars* was packed with an often-missing transparent and blue and gray *ray gun* and green tinted helmet. *Alpha 7* was sold on a colorful bubble blister card.

Alpha 7 - The Man from Mars

Item Name: **Electron+ The Man from Pluto**
Copyright Date: 1968
Accessories: *Ray Gun* and *Space Helmet*.
Details:

The Man from Pluto, *Electron+* was a silver, robotic-looking figure. He had the common accordion joints, as did all of the *Outer Space Men*. This bendie figure was molded in a gray rubber plastic and painted over in silver paint. *Electron+* was molded wearing tall, knee-high boots, and what appear to be elbow-length gloves. The *Man from Pluto* has an orange disk located in his chest area for added style. This figure was sold

with a blue tinted helmet and his ever-trusty orange and gray *ray gun*. Highly imaginative bubble card artwork showed an illustrated *Electron+* in an electromagnetic type of laboratory.

Electron+ - The Man from Pluto

Item Name: **Orbitron – The Man from Uranus**
Copyright Date: 1968
Accessories: *Ray Gun*.
Details:

Orbitron was a large pink molded Colorform *Outer Space Man* figure. This figure had very little paint detailing and was permitted to show is true color, a vibrant pink hue. Accordion joints were used for this alien and supported huge feet and extra long claw-type hands. *Orbitron* was molded with a very large head, which contained a very large brain and beak like mouth. The box artwork was highly colorful with an illustration of *Orbitron's* home planet Uranus. *Orbitron* could be seen, *ray gun* in hand, on a dusty alien moon. *Orbitron* was held to the card by a clear full-length body bubble.

Part 4 - Colorforms *Outer Space Men*

Orbitron - The Man from Uranus

Colossus Rex - The Man from Juptier

Item Name: ***Colossus Rex – The Man from Jupiter***

Copyright Date: 1968

Accessories: Blue Mace / Club.

Details:

The *Outer Space Man* from Jupiter, *Colossus Rex*, was a fierce looking and very solid Colorform alien. This physically espousing figure was molded in a dark green rubber with a great deal of body paint. A dark green painted body with blue metallic painted highlight, black belt with mauve trunks, and belt detailing completed this figure. He was not friendly looking, with white fanged teeth and deep black eyes. This figure, in many ways, resembles the *Creature From The Black Lagoon*. A finned head with prominent ears and spindled back completes the look of this creature. A logo of Jupiter was illustrated on the box as was *Rex* on a planetoid surrounded with what appears to be mushrooms. The mace was his accessory item, molded in a transparent purple color.

Item Name: ***Astro-Nautilus – The Man from Neptune***

Copyright Date: 1968

Accessories: Staff.

Details:

The *Man from Neptune* was an odd looking alien, probably the most non-humanoid looking figure designed for the *Outer Space Men* line of toys. This alien continued to use the accordion flexible joints found on the other Colorforms, but the legs are where the humanoid tendencies ended. *Astro-Nautilus*, as the name suggests, resembled a squid or octopus type creature. This figure was designed with a very large head and, rather than conventional arms, was given four long ribbed tentacles. This figure was molded from a purple rubber with deeper purple coloring added to both the torso and feet areas. He was sold with his accessory, a blue plastic three pronged staff. The cover card artwork, again elaborate, displayed *Astro-Nautilus* on what was thought to be his home planet of Neptune. He appears to command this realm and is depicted in a deep-sea city beneath Neptune's' stormy oceans. The cold blue planet of Neptune is realistically illustrated on the top right corner of the box artwork.

Part 4 - Colorforms *Outer Space Men*

Astro-Nautilus - The Man from Neptune

Commander Comet - The Man from Venus

Item Name: **Commander Comet – The Man from Venus**
Copyright Date: 1968
Accessories: Helmet, Crossbow and Wings.
Details:

Commander Comet was born on Venus. This figure appears to have been designed as a cross between a futuristic angel and an astronaut. The *Commander* wears large white wings that help him soar through the misty Venusion atmosphere. His helmet, molded in a light pink hue, lends to the notion of an astronaut rather than angel. The *Man from Venus* is painted gold in color. Beneath the body paint is a pink molded humanoid figure. *Commander Comet* was the only figure in the line that features a human head and face, and continues his human-like traits with arms, hands, legs and feet. Two small ringed mounts were molded into an area his torso just above his hips. Colorforms must have believed that if any of the *Outer Space Men* were going to fly, *Commander Comet*, with the presto wings, was be the one. The loop was to be used as the places to tie on string to allow him to soar through the heavens. The box artwork for this toy is particularly striking. Photos on the front of the box

show the *Commander* flying, wings outstretched, over a cloud city on Venus, a glowing orb in the foreground with hundreds of stars twinkling in the midnight sky. Another photo displays *Commander Comet*, with bow in hand, pointed towards the same starlit sky, standing among the Venetian clouds. This figure, when found, most often is missing the gold paint from his torso, similar to the silver paint that is frequently missing from *Electron+ - The Man from Pluto*. These two metallic-type paints don't appear to hold up very well over time and rub off with play.

Item Name: **Xodiac – The Man from Saturn**
Copyright Date: 1968
Accessories: Helmet, *Ray Gun* and Staff.
Details:

This *Outer Space Man from Saturn* was my favorite Colorforms toy as a child. *Xodiac* stood 6" in height, and was a perfect match for *Major Matt Mason*, in fact, his arms and legs appear to be almost an exact match in terms of size and design. Again, this Colorform was molded in colored rubber, this time bright red was used. He was a highly detailed figure, from his very alien head — wide brow, pointed chin, deep set slit eyes and long pointed ears — to a large upper chest, almost armored in nature. He was painted, for the most part, except head and accordion flex joints, in a deep metallic blue paint. He wore a mauve embossed and painted V shaped belt, and had an oval emblem on his chest. *Xodiac*, as with all Colorform Alien *Outer Space Men*, has printing and copyright information on his back — "R Colorforms" "Made in Hong Kong." The box art, again elaborate, had two very intriguing pictures. The first was *Xodiac* standing on his planet with pink staff accessory in one hand and pink *ray gun* in the other. The second photograph depicts *Xodiac* moving high over the red-rocked surface of Saturn by way of a futuristic type air balloon. As with all Colorform *Outer Space Men*, *Xodiac's* ringed home world of Saturn can be seen in the top right corner of the bubble card.

Xodiac - The Man from Saturn

Paper Products, Spin-Offs And Accessory Items

The Colorform Company didn't make only the seven terrific *Outer Space Men* three-dimensional bendie figures, they also made some very cool accessory items. As Ideal toys discovered with the reintroduction of the *Star Team* toys, Colorforms, with their *Outer Space Men*, enjoyed a renewed interest in space and science fiction in mid 1970's. *Star Wars* had hit a home run, the public was primed, and the cascading effect made everything space-related "hot"! Colorforms released the *Outer Space Men* again, not in a rubberized bendie format, although other Hong Kong companies were doing that, but in jigsaw puzzle and as what Colorforms were really known for, stick-on sets. Colorforms made a total of four puzzles. The photographs were taken from original bubble card artwork and had the second series *World of the Future Aliens* superimposed onto the photographs. Included here, you'll see *Orbitron* with *Cyclops* standing on a planetary surface. Another jigsaw puzzles shows *Electron+* standing in his laboratory accompanied by *Gemini – The Man from the Twin Star Algol* and *The Man from the*

Outer Space Men puzzles

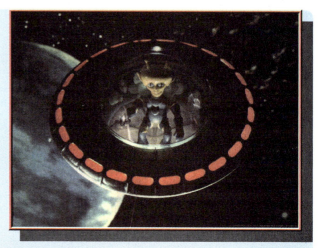

4th Dimension. The third jigsaw puzzle in the series shows *Colossus Rex* with *The Man from Saturn, Xodiac* and *Astro-Nautilus.* The final puzzle, and my personal favorite, is none other than *Alpha 7. Alpha 7* is the only *Alien* creature shown in a space ship, his one-man saucer, flying over the earth as it spins silently in the black void below. These puzzles were actually taken from the original bubble box artwork produced years earlier, of course, without the series two figures. The last paper item that was produced by Colorforms was the *Space Warriors Colorforms Playset,* copyright 1976. I remember being terribly disappointed when I got this item home from Simpsons-Sears. I thought that is was going to be an actual playset, rather than a stick-on set. Still it was very neat, showing both the *Outer Space Men* and the *World of the Future* spaced-out figures. These stickers could be placed and replaced in hundreds of action positions. This was a truly cool item, due primarily to the great box art, and being the only way that you could purchase both Series one and Series two toys together.

Outer Space Men playset (below and right)

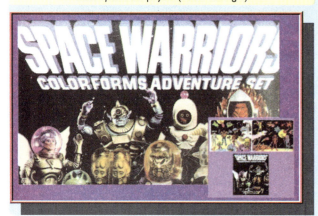

Box Art And Company Advertising

As discussed briefly in an earlier chapter, the Colorforms company, in designing their box graphics and text, combined real life, known space facts with other-worldly science fiction. The result was a unique individual character development for each of the Colorform *Outer Space Men* and *World of the Future* aliens. What follows has been taken directly from the bubble cards that the aliens were sold on, which, I believe, enhanced the play value of these toys greatly. Colorforms didn't exist in the real world and, unlike *Major Matt Mason,* who was directly linked to the NASA space program, Colorforms were out on a tenuous limb. They relied heavily on both imagery and a link with Mattel's line of toys, and became the aliens that the *Major Matt Mason* series of toys lacked, adding a science fiction twist to our toy play. The back side of each Colorform bubble card included the character development, history and planetoid information given below.

The *Outer Space Men* - Series One

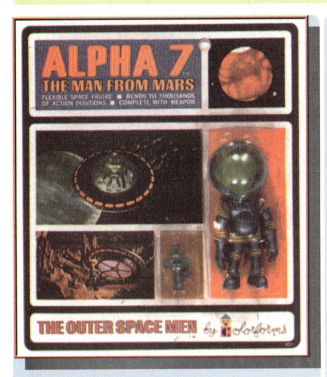

Alpha 7 – The Man from Mars
Far below the surface of the dying planet Mars, the descendants of a once great race live on. Above them the majestic cities have long since crumbled and the vast canals lie buried beneath a silent sea of rust red

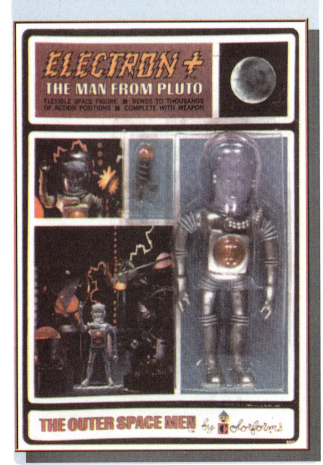

sand. With time and water running out, *Alpha 7* and the other member of the Martian armada travel the galaxy in search of a suitable planet to make their own. Their frequent reconnaissance missions and landings on our Earth have given rise to what most earth-men consider "wild" stories of "flying saucers" and "little green men."

Electron+ - The Man from Pluto
The cold and desolate planet of Pluto is too far from the sun to derive its heat and, thus, the very atmosphere lies frozen and life as we know it cannot exist. But there, at the very edge of our solar system, the great Intergalactic Winds that blow between the stars carry with them great masses of cosmic energy. In the beginning, this living energy bombarding the frozen planet did itself freeze to become living matter and, thus, a mighty race of beings began. Created of energy, they can become energy at will and *Electron+*, from his laboratory in Electra City, can transport himself throughout the universe as a beam of light.

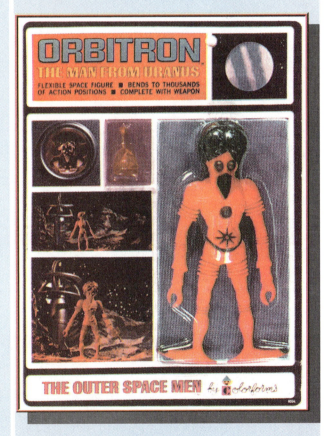

Orbitron – The Man from Uranus
From the barren mountains of Uranus great waves of thought reach-out through the blackness of outer space probing the universe. Thus, *Orbitron* and the men of Uranus search the stars seeking the list knowledge of the Ancient Ones. On great ships they travel to the farthest reaches of our galaxy and beyond. Able to read the minds of men, they have collected the learning of a

thousand worlds, and yet they go on searching in a never ending quest to learn that which is has been ordained no man shall ever know.

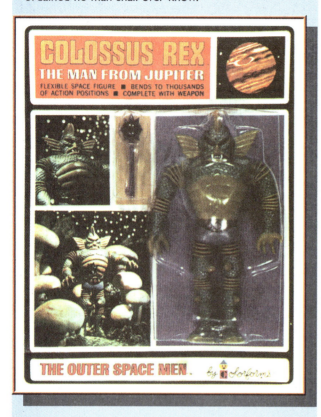

Colossus Rex – The Man from Jupiter
From the huge red spot near the equator of the giant planet Jupiter, a great ship travels forth. On board is the mighty warrior, *Colossus Rex*, strongest of the strong. The colossal strength needed merely to survive the crushing pressure of the atmosphere and enormous force of gravity on his native Jupiter make him a veritable superman on other worlds. Invulnerable to attack, invincible in battle, brute strength alone is his only weapon. Yet no power in the galaxy can defeat him. We hope his mission is merely to explore the universe and not to conquer it.

Astro-Nautilus – The Man from Neptune
Deep beneath the stormy seas of Neptune, great cities loom majestically in the shimmering twilight of a vast and beautiful water world. Here the mighty Triton people live. Not content to see the sun as a but a glimmer and the stars as tiny ripples floating on the surface of the sea above, *Astro-Nautilus* and his band of Triton mariners venture forth to sail and chart that greater ocean, Outer Space. Often visiting our planet they land, secretly, without all human knowledge, in the very depths of Earth's great oceans.

Commander Comet – The Man from Venus
From Olympus, the largest of the great cloud cities of Venus, the mighty cloud ship Cumulus sets forth. Like a fiery comet it blazes through the blackness of outer space toward Earth. Its captain, *Commander Comet*, is a direct descendant of the mighty Zeus, the leader of the

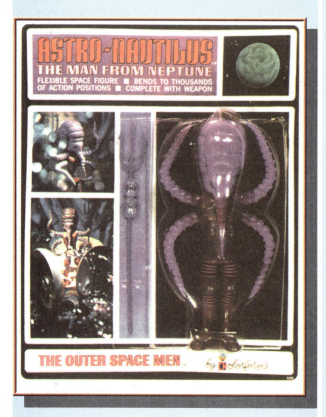

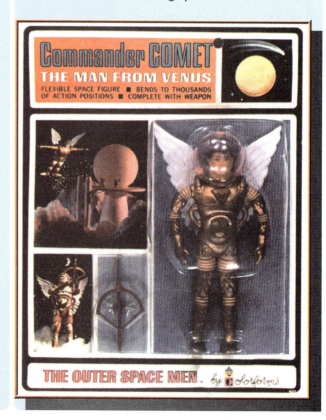

historic first Venusian expedition to Earth, which landed near the Grecian Isles 3,000 years ago. *Commander Comet*'s present mission is one of routine Earth surveillance, and once within the atmosphere of Earth, his ship will join the great fleet of Venusian craft that float like clouds above our planet night and day, watching undetected over our world.

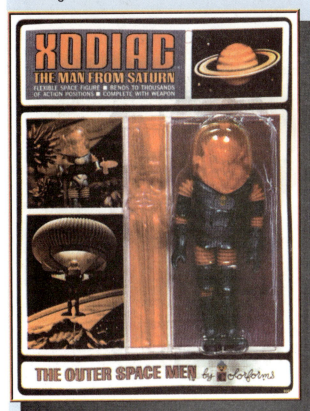

as stars! From a place so vast it cannot have a name, comes *CYCLOPS*, mighty intergalactic giant! Great Warrior of the Cosmos! In his forehead, the All-Seeing Eye, With it he can witness all that is happening anywhere in the universe. In his belt he carries two additional eyes. One can see the past, the other, the future. Gliding swiftly between the stars, through the

Xodiac – The Man from Saturn

Saturn is the most beautiful of all the planets. Its symmetrical rings give it a matchless grace and there is nothing like them anywhere else in the solar system. Constructed and placed in orbit by the Elders, millenniums ago, they give the people of Saturn complete mastery over the forces of gravity on their planet. Thus, all work is done by perpetual motion and men can fly above their world in great machines tuned to the frequency of the rings. Freed from manual labor, the men of Saturn have developed great wisdom and the wisest among them is *Xodiac*. It is said of him that he can tune his staff to play upon the great rings; the music of the spheres resounding throughout the universe to be heard by wise men everywhere.

The World Of The Future - Series Two

Cyclops – Giant beyond the Milky Way

Beyond the stars and star smoke of our Milky Way! Out past the shining citadels of other galaxies as numerous

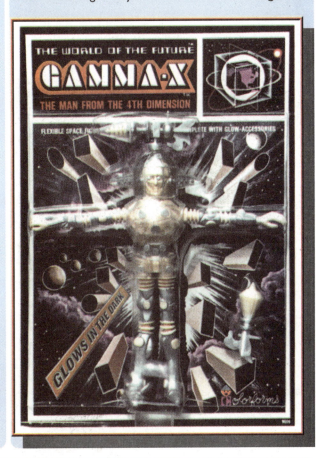

darkest reaches of intergalactic space, he travels throughout eternity, forever seeking "more than meets the eye"

Gamma-X – The Man from the 4th Dimension

Although we cannot see it, the world of the 4th dimension is all around us. Right here and now! But in a different plane and dimension. *GAMMA X*, by activating his Time and Space Materializer, is able to break through into our 3-dimensional world and make himself visible to us! Like the many 4-dimensional beings who have visited our world before him, he is able to walk through what we regard as solid walls, appear and disappear at will, and seemingly defy the laws of gravity. Throughout history, mankind has tried in vain to explain these visitors from another dimension by falsely attributing to them some supernatural origin, never realizing that the being we call "ghosts" are really *Men of the 4th Dimension*.

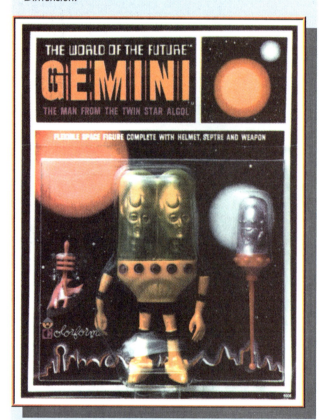

Gemini – The Man from the twin star ALGOL

High above the roof of our world, the twin star Algol — in reality, two stars, a massive Red Giant and a Blue-White Dwarf — shines its double light upon its only planet, the tiny world of "Mu." Its inhabitants, through small in physical stature, are said to possess the greatest intellect in the universe and many of them have mastered the power of the mind over matter. Thus *GEMINI* has built great cities by merely "thinking" them to be, and through the power of thought alone, created

the Majestic Ship in which he crosses the voids of outer space to visit other worlds.

Inferno – The Flame Man of Mercury

On Mercury, the planet nearest our Sun, great rivers of molten metal churn and flow past majestic cities, glowing red hot in the blinding radiance of the Sun. Here, in temperatures so great that life as we know it would be consumed in a flash, the mighty Volcan Peoples live — beings of living fire that burn eternally. Protected by suits of thermal alloy, lest the freezing cold of outer space should snuff them out, *INFERNO* and the *Men of Mercury* travel the universe in the great chariots of fire that we call comets.

Metamorpho – The Man from Alpha Centauri

Able to transform himself at will, *METAMORPHO* set forth many centuries ago from the third Satellite of the great star, Alpha Centauri, to explore the universe. By taking on the physical characteristics of the inhabitants of the different worlds he visits, he is able to walk unnoticed among them and study their ways. In his travels he has changed himself into many wild and alien forms that he has long ago forgotten what his own was like. Thus, *METAMORPHO* has come to know all the strange and wonderful beings in the universe and to understand the "oneness" of all life everywhere.

Mystron – The Man from Hollow Earth

Often, men exploring the deepest caves and caverns of the Earth have disappeared, never to be seen again. But freezing Arctic temperatures and Magnetic Force Shields have successfully prevented mankind from discovering the really major entrances to *Hollow Earth*, the giant doorways located directly at the North and South Poles. It is through these giant openings that *MYSTRON* and *The Men of Hollow Earth* guide their winged ships whose awkward flapping stirs up vast Arctic winds that engulf our world as they struggle to leave the heavy atmosphere of Earth and reach the smooth ether on which to glide to distant stars.

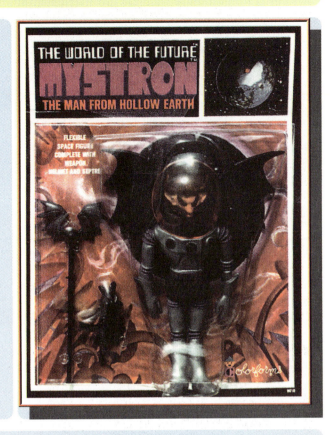

Outer Space Men Price Guide

I'm sure that you will find this price section controversial and may disagree with some pricing. It's my hope you'll also find pricing that will surprise you. Colorforms have seen tremendous growth in collectability over the last few years and prices continue to rise rapidly. The prices that are shown reflect the current prices that you can expect to pay for the *Outer Space Men*. As in the value sections of both *Major Matt Mason* and *Zeroids*, the values here are based on dealer asking prices at toy shows, from printed sources such as toy collectable publications, and internet auction houses. As with any collectable item, the value is directly related to the intrinsic value that a prospective collector places on the item. Yes, there will be times when you stumble across a toy which should command high prices in the marketplace but is priced low. This is especially true of Colorforms, and many sellers are not educated and so do not know, or will not recognize, Colorforms *Outer Space Men*. They don't have a history of collectability in the same way that *Major Matt Mason* has. Due to their scarcity, they are not as well known or as easily recognized by most. Further, supply and demand is most often the determining factor for pricing any collectable toy, along with the second most important factor for determining price, complete and original boxes, packaging and instructions. It is, as I've stated before, at the discretion of the buyer and the willingness of the seller to arrange an agreeable price for a particular toy. The prices that I've provided in this reference guide are the prices that you should expect to pay to buy an item. They are not necessarily what you can expect to receive when you are selling the same toy to a toy dealer, in fact, you should expect about fifty percent of the guide price when selling to a dealer.

Colorform Toy Values

How To Use This Colorform Reference Guide:

This page contains prices for both loose and carded Colorform *Outer Space Men*. You'll note that the toys have a value in both the MOC (Mint on Card) and the loose categories. I have also complied a list of values for toy accessories that are off the card and can be found loose, without the original Colorform *Outer Space Man*.

Outer Space Men: Colorform Toys 1968-1970

Alien	Loose / Fair	Loose / Excellent	Good / Carded
Astro-Nautilus	85.00	350.00	600.00
Orbitron	45.00	100.00	350.00
Colossus Rex	75.00	275.00	500.00
Electron+	45.00	100.00	350.00
Alpha 7	30.00	75.00	300.00
Commander Comet	85.00	250.00	500.00
Xodiac	45.00	200.00	450.00

Loose Accessories

If you are fortunate, and have a good eye, you may locate Colorform *Outer Space Men* accessories. The Colorform company included tiny, but nifty, *ray guns*, helmets and staffs with most of their Alien bendie figures. As a general rule, accessory *ray guns* and staffs in good condition will sell for about $20.00 each. Helmets are much dearer in price, and a good helmet can fetch upwards of $40.00 each. It's almost impossible to locate a near mint helmet because of the chemical reaction that occurs between the rubber antenna on *Xodiac* and *Alpha 7* and the hard plastic of their helmets.

Series Two: *The World Of The Future*

"An Aborted Liftoff" Product Line

The first and only true production set or "official" Colorforms were produced in 1968. This series of toys was produced in Hong Kong for short of two years. They were, by all accounts, a resounding success for the Colorforms company. As a result, *Series Two: The World Of The Future* was designed, through to the production phase. Figures were designed and molded, accessories manufactured, display bubble cards were even put together, but, it is reported, only five complete sets were ever produced as prototype figures / cards. It's estimated that only two complete sets actually survive today, some thirty years later.

If the first set of seven figures was highly acclaimed for their imaginative designs, both illustratively and with great production values, the planned *Series Two* figures were out of this world. "From Beyond Tomorrow Comes the World of the Future" proclaimed Colorforms in their early publicity planning for *Series Two*. Box artwork for each was even more daring than with *Series One*, more accessories, wilder designs, exciting illustrations, and now battery operation (not unlike our friend *Scorpio*) was now going to be added. Each of the six figures had individual information (at increased production costs) on its bubble card.

The new aliens were, for the most, not part of our solar system, however, the *Series One* exclusions had now been added. Who were the new aliens that Colorforms had planned to produce? None other than *Cyclops – The Giant from beyond the Milky Way, Gamma-X – The Man from the Forth Dimension, Gemini – The Man from the twin star ALGOL, Inferno – The Flame Man from Mercury, Metamorpho – The Man from Alpha Centauri*, and finally, *Mystron – The Man from Hollow Earth*. These figures, as with the *Major Matt Mason* toys and earlier Colorform aliens, continued to be molded from a pliable rubber compound molded over a wire metal skeletal framework.

In the first series of toys, all figures were sold with accessories, such as *ray gun* weapons, maces, helmets and *cosmic staffs*. *Series Two: The World of the Future* figures were to be sold with accessories as well including, gold plated body armor, glow in the dark accessories, helmets, septres and laser weapons. The new *World of the Future* figures, it was planned, would add a new dimension of play value. Not only would these figure bend into "thousands of action positions" like their series one cousins, but now they were getting properties unique to themselves. Each was planned to be sold on individually labeled and beautifully illustrated bubble display cards with unique action.

Item Name: *Cyclops – Giant beyond the Milky Way*

Accessories: Space weapon, space Helmet and space Armor.

Details:

Cyclops was a large figure with a green and blue painted body. He shares many of the styling cues originally seen on *Colossus Rex* - the same large upper body, similar head, and same molded claw hands. The *Giant* was molded in purple rubber compound, which only showed thorough on hands, accordion joints and the abdominal area. His line of accessories included his weapon and huge body armor with integrated helmet. This two piece design snapped over the upper torso of *Cyclops* exposing only his arms and legs. The design shared these traits with the similarly operating *Moon Suit* which was designed to snap over *Major Matt Mason*. The *Giant beyond the Milky Way* was shown on his prototype card with a basic star background. In the topmost right corner was a small illustration of the Milky Way.

Item Name: *Gamma-X – The Man from the 4th Dimension*

Accessories: *Ray Gun* weapon and *4th dimension wand.*

Details:

The Man from the 4th Dimension is my favorite *Series Two* figure. The box is beautifully illustrated showing purple clouds in outer space with many worlds and monolith-type structures floating around *Gamma X*. This figure looks to be a cross between the *Tin Man* from the *Wizard of Oz* and a first series *Electron+*. Jointed shoulders, elbows legs and knees enabled *Gamma-X* to pose. His yellow rubber cast body with silver painted detailing looks quite striking. His unique feature was that you could hold him up to a light source and charge him up — then turn off the lights, and he glows. His accessories were planned to glow as well, being made of the same type of rubber compound.

Gamma-X - The Man from the 4th Dimension

Item Name: *Gemini – The Man from the Twin Star ALGOL*

Accessories: *Space Ray Gun, Space Septre* and Helmet.

Details:

Gemini – The Man from the Twin Star ALGOL was the strangest alien from *Series Two*. This figure was a smallish figure. Yellow arms and legs, very human-like, were designed for this figure. That's where the human comparison ends. Our twin star man had two twin-alien heads, which were very long, with pointed noses and chins. They were housed inside an equally large double helmet. There was little detailing to the body as a whole, other than black molding at accordion

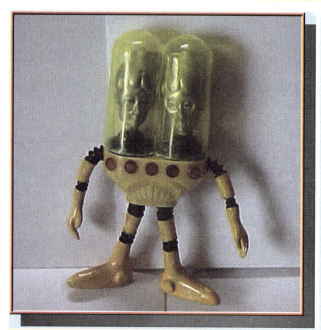

Gemini – The Man from the Twin Star ALGOL

joints and what appeared to be a row of lights just under the helmet area. The *Man from the Twin Star* system was to have been sold with some very cool looking space gear, including his red *Space Ray Gun* and red septre. Box artwork was somewhat more generic for this figure, with a line drawn cityscape, and, to the bottom of the card, a midnight black sky, and large bright orange planet in the upper most left corner. If this figure was as Colorform claimed "The World of the Future", then things were going to be getting pretty strange.

Item Name: ***Inferno – The Flame Man***
                  of Mercury
Accessories: Flame head and Helmet.
Details:

The *World of the Future*'s *Inferno* figure would have been a first for Colorforms. Similar in concept to the *Scorpio* figure created for Mattel's *Major Matt Mason: Man in Space* series, *Inferno* would light up. Colorforms had planned to include this battery operated figure in the *Series Two* line up. Press an orange button located on *Inferno*'s chest and watch *Inferno*'s flame like face light up. *Inferno*'s helmet could be removed and replaced with a another helmet with a flame molded at the top, which would also light up. This figure was a silver looking humanoid and shared design similarities with *Xodiac* from *Series One* — similar type chest with embossed lightening bolt and torso were the primary crossover ideas. Of course, like all Colorforms produced, he came with the mandatory flex joints. Box artwork featured a futuristic orange planetoid with black starred lined sky. The box artwork stated that this figure was a "Flexible space figure complete with helmet and

light-up flame head." A large plastic flame was planned for inclusion, which like *Commander Comet*'s wings, could be attached to *Inferno*'s back.

Item Name: ***Metamorpho – The Man***
                  from Alpha Centauri
Accessories: Accessory space unit, Ray gun, Gold transforming face, Red transforming face and Alpha Centauri face.
Details:

The Man from Alpha Centauri was a humanoid looking figure for the most part. Larger than average chest, with thin legs and arms painted in stark white were the significant features of this toy. Black rubber joints and brief area were the only black areas on this figure. A red button was located in the middle of his chest. *Metamorpho* came with a unique helmet that included a knob at the top. The box artwork provided the instructions "turn knob to activate TRANSFORMAGIC HEAD identifies change instantly." Three accessory faces were included with this toy. There was an *Alpha Centauri*-type face, painted in both black and white, which matched the *World of the Future* figure nicely. This face looked similar to the *Space Ghost* cartoon figure head. Two additional faces were included — one was a gold alien with spiked hair, and the other a red faced alien with large eyes and fangs. Two additional accessory items were planned for this item as well. Both looked like space-age defensive equipment, one being a *ray gun*. Box artwork was highly colorful with the figure's name printed in rainbow colors. Located in the upper right corner was a picture of the far off Alpha Centauri star cluster.

Mystron – The Man from Hollow Earth

Item Name:	**Mystron – The Man from Hollow Earth**
Accessories:	Weapon, Helmet and Septre.

Details:

This figure filled in the missing planets of our solar system from *Series One* of Colorform aliens. *Mystron* was an evil-looking figure with large bat wings, bat-like septre and ray gun. The figure itself was painted in a dark silverish coloring. *Mystron* has legs similar to *Inferno*, with a large, square and broad chest area. *Mystron* was molded in purple rubber, which showed through at the accordion joints and lower torso. I think this was the most interesting head designed of the *Series Two* prototypes. The creature was molded with long hair, slanted evil eyes and pointed ears. Horns were molded into the top of his head. *Mystron* wore a red hued helmet, which was shaped in an oval design much like *Commander Comet's* helmet from *Series One*. Packaging for this figure was bright orange and red illustrations made to look like the center of the earth. *Mystron* was an extremely imaginative and mysterious looking figure, with demonic styling and design influences. It's a shame that this figure wasn't produced past the prototype stage.

Colorforms Knock-Offs — Another Hong Kong Connection

. . . goes back to the late 1960's — 1968 through 1970 — when the first edition of knock-off (unlicensed) Colorform *Outer Space Men* aliens was produced. The knock-offs, and there were many, have carried on for many, many years. The first miniature set of six aliens was very small — only about 2" in height. *Alpha 7, Electron+, Orbitron, Xodiac, Commander Comet* and *Colossus Rex* were produced. They remained very true to the original Colorform *Outer Space Men*, right down to their accessory weapons. They were not of the same relative proportions as he originals, however — *Alpha 7* was now the same height as *Colossus Rex*, for example. These aliens were sold both in gumball machines (in those little eggs), and, more interestingly, on bubble cards, two per pack. These bootleg *Outer Space Men* were called *Space Marauder Bendables* and sold for a hefty 59 cents! The bubble card stated that these *Space Marauders* were "strange NU Landings from the Outer Limits of the Universe." These aliens by Toy House advertised that the buyer could "twist em, bend em and shape em."

Space Marauders bendables from Toy House

Various *Outer Space Men* knock-offs varied considerably in size

This second knock-off set was only 1" to 2" hgh

The second series of very tiny *Outer Space Men* was made in the early half of the 1970's. These 1" to 2" tall, hard black or gray plastic molded figures were true to the original molds, but were, again, produced in Hong Kong. Only six in the series were made, *Astro-Nautilus* was excluded from this set of bootleg toys.

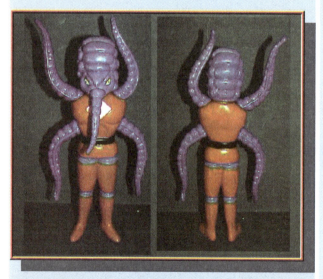

At about this time, another knock-off line of *Outer Space Men* was made — the very rare and expensive Bullmark *Outer Space Men*. These figures did differ more in details than previous Colorform rip-offs. The coloring

The very rare Bullmark *Outer Space Men* (above, below and left)

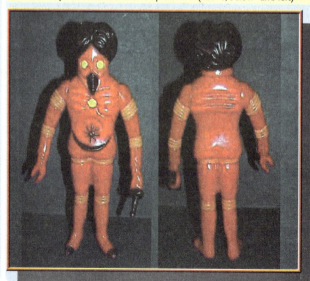

Part 4 - Colorforms *Outer Space Men*

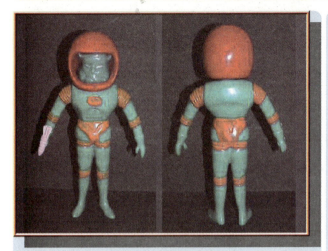

Another rare Bullmark *Outer Space Man*

on these was not the same as the originals, and helmets were larger and not clear see through plastic as were the originals.

The forth series of *Outer Space Men* was sold in 1996. These too are rare and hard to find. Again, *Astro-Nautilus* is the odd man out. These figures, standing a couple of inches in height, were molded in silver or black hard plastic, and they're stamped "Made in China." The coloring of these little guys is pretty horrendous, and all but *Xodiac* and *Colossus Rex* have red boots. A considerable amount of gold accent paint was used on each figure — *Alpha 7*'s head, *Colossus Rex*'s chest and ears, and *Commander Comet*'s wings, to name a few. The main body and appendages are colored silver, with red or blue gloves painted on most figures. Each figure has the accessory *ray gun*, mace, or staff molded onto the figure. Finally, these final figures were sold on colorful blister cards, two at a time, packaged with three bootleg ships from the old Gerry Anderson *Thunderbirds* marionette series of the early 1960's.

The fourth *Outer Space Men* copies had a horrendous paint job

The fourth set was sold on blister cards along with space ships

It truly is a credit to the one of the most endearing, most artistically creative toy lines of the 1960's that, almost thirty years after the fact, they continue to be popular enough to be reproduced yet one more time.

Part 4 - Colorforms *Outer Space Men*

Colorforms - A Cottage Industry Is Born

In this chapter I'll explore the use of the world wide Internet in providing reproduction accessory items for Colorforms Alien *Outer Space Men*. An acquaintance friend of mine writes:

Outer Space Men accessories

"Welcome fellow space travelers. This project to reproduce accessories for the Colorforms *Outer Space Men* line of Alien figures was primarily born out of frustration. Although many of these imaginative figures have survived for over thirty years, sadly, their weapons and accessories have not. Actually finding an elusive Colorform Alien with a weapon or *Space Helmet* intact is a rare and expensive event. Most of these Aliens will display quite nicely in a collection as they are, however, *Commander Comet* in particular, lacks a certain flair without his wings and thus began my quest to acquire or borrow original accessories for the purposes of reproducing them for myself and other collectors. The original weapons and helmets appear to have been injection molded in rigid tinted, transparent styrene; the exception being *Commander Comet's* Bow and Wings, which is solid plastic.

To make reproductions of the accessories, molds were taken of the originals. The accessories are not mass-produced by any means as each individual weapon is cast separately and requires further work when it has cured and is removed from the mold."

While Mattel's *Major Matt Mason* figures are of the same vintage and similar in construction as our *Outer Space Men*, Mattel's astronaut hands are still very flexible and have somehow retained their ability to hold the accessories supplied with them. Unfortunately, the Colorform Aliens are sadly lacking in this characteristic. The distance between the thumb and fingers on most figures appears too great to firmly grasp the *Ray Guns*, even with the aid of the spike that's molded onto the butt of their weapons. The problem is further compounded by the fact that the rubber that they're made from has hardened a little over the years. Most items are available including *Alpha 7's* ray gun, *Astro-Nautilus's* trident, *Colossus Rex's* mace, *Commander Comet's* wings, *Electron+'s* ray gun and chest emblem, and *Xodiac's* cosmic staff and ray gun. More accessory reproduction items are currently being planned. If you would like more information on these items, please visit Graeme on his web site on the Internet at http://home.interhop.net/~grwalker/cgi-bin/cfaintro.htm.

Part 4 - Colorforms *Outer Space Men*

Long before those other Storm Troopers . . .

Part 4 - Colorforms *Outer Space Men*

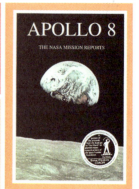

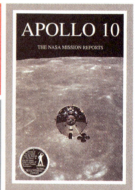